And You Call This F-ing Leadership?

A case study on leadership chronicling the demise of
FedEx National LTL

Steven H. Newhouse

"The growth and development of people is the highest calling of leadership."
Harvey Firestone - founder of Firestone Tire and Rubber

Copyright © 2013 Steven H. Newhouse

All rights reserved.

ISBN-10: 1483917878

ISBN-13: 978-1483917870

DEDICATION

****

"Teamwork is the ability to work together toward a common vision. The ability to direct individual accomplishment toward organizational objectives. It is the fuel that allows common people to attain uncommon goals." - Andrew Carnegie - founder of Carnegie Steel Company (U.S. Steel)

This book is dedicated to the thousands of employees and contract drivers who devoted many years of their working lives to building Watkins Motor Lines, Inc. into a highly successful and well respected national transportation company. Every day of my 15 years working at Watkins Motor Lines I was surrounded by people who truly enjoyed coming to work every day. They accepted each other as equal members of the team and respected their unique differences. They believed in going above and beyond to ensure a positive customer experience every day. They performed their jobs because they wanted to, not because they had to. They had fun and took their jobs seriously, but not themselves. It was fun coming to work. Everybody considered themselves as part of a very successful team. These hard working individuals defined for me, in watching them interact with each other day in and day out, the true meaning of "teamwork" and what can be accomplished by a workforce committed to "working together."

****

"Coming together is a beginning; keeping together is progress; working together is success." - Henry Ford - founder of Ford Motor Company

CONTENTS

Acknowledgments - vii

Introduction - xi

1. Why The Title? - 2

2. The History and Culture of Watkins Motor Lines - - - - - 6

3. The Evolution of FedEx Freight - - - - - - - - - - - - - - - - 24

4. The Asset Acquisition - 32

5. The American Freightways Bias - - - - - - - - - - - - - - - - 46

6. A Very Short Honeymoon - - - - - - - - - - - - - - - - - - - 56

7. Transmogrification Begins - - - - - - - - - - - - - - - - - - - 70

8. Transmogrification Continues - - - - - - - - - - - - - - - - 88

9. The Dark Days Get Even Darker - - - - - - - - - - - - - - - 106

10. The Dawn of a New Era - 122

11. Discovering The Real FedEx - - - - - - - - - - - - - - - - - 140

12. The Points of Leadership - - - - - - - - - - - - - - - - - - - 150

Retrospective - 163

ACKNOWLEDGMENTS

****

"It is not so much our friend's help that helps us, as the confidence of their help."
Epicurus - ancient Greek philosopher

I start by thanking **Al Lucia**, founder of ADL Associates, Inc. a nationwide network of speakers, consultants and trainers dedicated to providing business executives with customized solutions to today's people challenges. Al has co-authored nine books, including the best-selling "Walk the Talk," "The Street Savvy Leader," and the highly popular "Leadership Secrets of Santa Claus." Al, a good friend for many years, sat with me several years ago and encouraged me to write a book - he said he felt I had a message within me and when the time was right, I would know what to write about with passion and conviction.

I also owe a tremendous thanks to **Rose Ann Froberg**, retired director and senior manager of Employee Communications at Watkins Motor Lines and FedEx National LTL, who worked by my side for almost 20 years. She is a gifted communicator, trusted confidant and friend who consistently provided objective, straight forward, and timely employee communications and information to thousands of employees and contract drivers across the country. In writing this book, she has provided me with invaluable insights and editorial suggestions.

I have had the words "show me, don't tell me your story" pounded into my head by my trusted friend, **Wendy Amengual Wark**, founder and president of Inclusion Strategy, a NYC based consulting firm dedicated to the transformative inclusion that drives both greater innovation and market share among a variety of Fortune 500 corporations and non-profit organizations. Her guidance and insights have kept me focused on telling this compelling account.

I am also thankful for the advice and friendship of **Barney Barnhardt**, who describes himself as a self employed, somewhat retired attorney, mediator and legal consultant since 1998, following a 29 year career as a corporate and securities attorney and partner of a large prestigious law firm in North Carolina. Barney has provided invaluable editing and counsel to ensure that my story and examples were objective and fact based. I found his experience and insights into the trucking industry, coupled with his legal perspectives and advice, critically important.

This book also would not have been possible without the help of numerous friends from both inside, as well as, outside the trucking industry. And a special thanks to those from both Watkins Motor Lines and FedEx National LTL who provided their input and perspectives from their own journey through the time lines and key events during our years together. Everyone who has helped me with this project has been inspirational and encouraged me to share this case study and the countless lessons learned.

I save my most heartfelt thanks for my wife, **Cheryl**, and our two children, **Grant and Becca**, all three of whom have been my greatest supporters. Cheryl has been my primary inspiration to complete this book for it is she that understands, on a personal level, the impact that inadequate leadership can have on an individual, on a loved one, on a family, on a workforce and on a company. She has always encouraged me and supported my goals. She has made me a better person for which I can never thank her enough.

****

"The language of friendship is not words, but meanings."
Henry David Thoreau - author, poet, philosopher.

INTRODUCTION

****

"If your actions inspire others to dream more, learn more, do more and become more, you are a leader." - John Quincy Adams - Sixth President of the United States

If you are reading this book, or being required to read it by a teacher, instructor, consultant, or someone in management, it is because you or they have a sincere interest in what really constitutes effective leadership. Reading this book will give you insights into what good leadership is and provide examples on how far ineffective leadership can let a good company fall.

During my 43-year career in Human Resources management I have worked under many different leaders and leadership styles. My journey has provided me with a thorough exposure to and understanding of various disciplines within the Human Resources function - employee relations, labor relations, compensation, benefits, staffing, training, employee communications, safety, employee engagement, etc. My career has relocated me to seven states (some two or more times), and eleven cities (some twice) working for seven different corporations plus serving two years of active duty as an Adjutant and Personnel Officer in an Air Defense Artillery Battalion in the US Army in Germany. My work with employees and management from missile sites, to production plants, to retail stores, to distribution centers, to freight docks, and through assignments in seven different corporate headquarters environments has given me a true appreciation for and understanding of the workforce at all levels and the importance of effective leadership. Throughout my career I have reported to 23 different individuals including directly reporting to eight different presidents. I have witnessed both good and inadequate leadership from the bottom up and have a true appreciation on how it can affect a workforce and a business.

I have been fortunate to have had these work experiences in four different industries - the military, consumer packaged goods, retail and trucking. These industries are indeed very different and are made up of leaders, managers and employees unique to each. Over these past four decades, deep immersions in countless experiences have provided me with battle tested instincts and hard learned lessons on the leadership and management of employees in almost every conceivable work setting and corporate operating challenge.

Some have asked me why I wanted to write a book and case study on leadership when there are already thousands devoted to this subject. Simply put, I think I have something to offer. This is a corporate experience I lived and feel very passionate about the lessons that can be learned from it.

The four years at FedEx National LTL, near the end of my 43-year career, was a gut wrenching journey down a corporate highway that proved to be a devastating dead end for thousands of employees thanks to the combination of a weak economy and inadequate leadership.

In 2006, the FedEx Corporation acquired the assets of Watkins Motor Lines. I was the Watkins' VP of Human Resources at the time. With the acquisition, FedEx branded the assets of Watkins Motor Lines, Inc. to FedEx National LTL. By 2010, the trip down a highway that began with high hopes and aspirations was littered with broken promises, countless disappointments and the final heartbreaking demise of what had been a 74 year old, $1 billion profitable carrier just before the buyout.

What the FedEx National LTL workforce went through in those four years made me realize that it was time for me to share some of my personal insights into effective leadership and my perspectives on the critical importance of valuing workplace cultures.

What happened to the Watkins Motor Lines workforce once it became FedEx National LTL should never have happened, but it did; and, if by reading this book, you have a better understanding of what it means to be an effective leader to your workforce and what it takes to become the leader for whom you yourself would want to work, then I consider it well worth the time I spent writing it.

****

"If I read a book that cost me $20 and I get one good idea, I've gotten one of the greatest bargains of all time." - Tom Peters - *American writer on business practices*

Chapter 1

WHY THE TITLE?

****

"If you would not be forgotten, as soon as you are dead and rotten, either write things worth reading, or do things worth the writing." - Benjamin Franklin - one of the Founding Fathers of the United States

Some of my friends asked me how I picked the title for this book. The answer is simple; during my time with the FedEx Freight family of companies, I often found myself shaking my head and thinking those exact words. In my entire career, I had never experienced so many examples of such inadequate leadership in one place.

I also believe that it is important to give those not familiar with the trucking industry some additional perspective through the title. The nature of the trucking business is such that it places high demands on those in it and it tends to attract tough, strong-willed, independent men and women who don't suffer fools well. In the trucking industry, you learn early on that time is money and truckers don't mince words when their time is wasted. And nothing wastes time like inadequate leadership.

The lessons on leadership throughout this book are as much about what not to do as a leader as they are about what to do. Based on documented events, this is a chronicle of how FedEx Freight bungled the acquisition of Watkins Motor Lines so badly that after only four years, FedEx National LTL (aka Watkins Motor Lines), ceased to exist. I am the first to state that no company, however successful or admired as it may be, is immune from the mistakes of inadequate leaders. All large corporations make mistakes, even FedEx. What is important to me is what can be learned from those mistakes.

This narrative walks you through the four post-acquisition years that damaged and forever altered the lives of a workforce of almost 10,000 employees and contractors. Yes, during those initial years with FedEx Freight, I often thought - **"And You Call This F-ing Leadership?"** Some of the events sound almost like fiction and some are hard to believe, especially in a corporation like FedEx. Believe me, this is not a book of theory on leadership, this is the real thing. You just can't make this stuff up!

****

"If you have knowledge, let others light their candles with it." - *Winston Churchill - British Prime Minister, historian and writer*

And You Call This F-ing Leadership?

ND You Call This F-ing Leadership?

Chapter 2

THE HISTORY AND CULTURE OF WATKINS MOTOR LINES

****

"The development of Watkins Motor Lines was not that of acquiring large vehicles and property or that of large investment, but rather the coming together of numbers of capable, dedicated people; both the company employees and contracting owners and their drivers - all with the common goal in mind and a genuine concern for one another, which has led us to the success we enjoy."
Bill "BW" Watkins, founder of Watkins Motor Lines and Watkins Associated Industries.

To appreciate the culture of a 74-year old company, one must first understand its rich history of innovative growth, the people who devoted their lives to building the organization, and the culture that made it thrive. It is also important to understand that that same 74 year old company was considered by many to have been the best place to work in their entire careers. I am about to relate much of the Watkins Motor Lines history that was written in an article in the late 1980s by Rose Ann Froberg, Watkins director of Employee Communications in collaboration with the founder, Bill "BW" Watkins.

BW grew up on his family's farm in Metcalf, GA, and in the early 1930s while he was taking chickens to the market in Atlanta, he saw the possibilities of trucking as a viable business. So, after graduating high school, he acted on his idea and used his $300 nest egg to buy the first Watkins truck. Initially he was involved in buying, selling, and hauling produce, pecans, live and dressed poultry and eggs to Jacksonville, FL.

Three months later, the first little three-quarter ton Dodge was traded in for a two-ton Dodge with a 20-foot Dorsey stake-body trailer. From there the "fleet" soon grew to seven. "The drivers were my friends and neighbors...we were seeing the eastern part of the United States, having a good time, working hard and trying our best to cover the monthly truck payments, repair bills and gas," BW said.

It was also at this point that BW learned what he calls "that ever-familiar lesson to all truckers -- to operate a fleet of trucks, the owner must stay out of the driver's seat and apply all energies to getting the loads and managing the affairs of the business." Managing that business was not easy since the country was in the midst of the Great Depression. BW said, "I borrowed from neighbors, my father, and got all the money the Commercial Bank of Thomasville, GA, would let me have. The standard operating procedure was rushing to the bank every day with collections to cover checks coming into the bank; and quite often not digging up enough cash to cover them all; so establishing sound credit was a long time coming."

In 1935 the Motor Carrier Act was enacted and the ICC (Interstate Commerce Commission) was established to direct the transportation industry. The act, in essence, regulated interstate commerce by requiring shippers to have federal approval to haul certain commodities to and from specific locations. The act, designed to protect carriers from competition, also allowed the ICC to setup very strict rate schedules. These approvals, commonly referred to as authorities, required extensive documentation so the process was not only time consuming, it was also costly for the carriers.

By the mid-1930s, the company -- then known as Watkins Produce Company, Inc. -- had grown to about 40 trucks; but, because the law now required truck lines to have authority to haul certain loads on certain lanes, a second company was established - Watkins Motor

Lines, Inc. For a while, the two companies ran side-by-side trading, trafficking, and hauling loads that complemented each other.

Right around 1940, BW moved to a permanent shop and office on Cassidy Road in Thomasville, GA. That site remained the company's headquarters until it moved to Lakeland, FL, in 1966. When World War II began in 1941, the fleet had grown to about 50 trucks and operations at the new facilities adjusted to the times.

It was also a time of little revenue growth. The company entered the war years with approximately $50,000 net worth of capital and surplus, and came out four years later with about the same because the government strictly controlled wages and shipping rates.

To support the war effort, BW and the company's lawyer moved rapidly and within a period of 18 months, they had acquired more than 100 temporary authorities that allowed Watkins to haul just about any type of war material between Atlanta, Norfolk and the other military bases that ranged from Quonset Point, RI, to Pensacola, FL, to New Orleans, LA.

The fleet was "scattered over the Eastern seaboard; and, boy what a nightmare for maintenance and safety procedure enforcement....Tire and gasoline rationing was very tight; but, because of our military support involvement, we were allotted all that was needed, but oh the 'red tape' and hard work," according to BW.

After WWII ended, Watkins struck out in a new direction and began hauling perishables by acquiring the authorities to transport processed foods; primarily meats, dairy products and frozen foods. Along with the authorities, Watkins also bought several companies, that allowed expansion into the Midwest. One of the companies was in Waterloo, Iowa. It was used as the home base for hauling meat from principal packing plants in Iowa, Minnesota, Nebraska and Kansas.

In 1959, Watkins became the first commercial trucking company to serve Alaska. The truck that made the historic trip left Minneapolis and arrived in Anchorage in less than 94 hours. It carried 38,000 lbs. of fresh and frozen meat.

When the citrus frozen concentrate industry was born in the late 1940s, Watkins became a prime carrier, having obtained the rights to ship from Florida to the entire Midwest. BW wrote, "Beginning in 1950, we really started growing.... we set our goal to reach 100 trucks; we made that sometime during 1951."

BW added: "We were bringing in new people at a rapid pace -- both management personnel and contracting owners. With the contracting owners being the 'cornerstone' of our ability to grow and offer superior service."

The primary lanes for the frozen citrus products were between points in the Southeast and the Midwest, but by the mid-1950s, Watkins had also acquired the authority to transport it to New York, New Jersey, Pennsylvania and connecting points in New England.

Also at about that time, Watkins began building a solid management organization and practices. "We really got serious with our costing, accounting, safety work, and we established a really active traffic department...Watkins became the leader in publishing heavier minimums aimed at providing more dollar revenue per truck and per mile," BW said.

In the late 1950s the uniform weight laws allowed full use of tandem tractors and trailers. "We all were pushing for heavier and better paying loads. We had acquired frozen and perishable authorities to and from California and had an office there. Texas was also becoming an important state to Watkins, and we were really coming of age.....We had created a successful and aggressive image, and we were out to fulfill it. We all expected great things of ourselves," he said.

In the 1960s, Watkins matured as a hybrid trucking outfit and became one of the largest carriers of perishables in the country. It had split its business between two divisions; one strictly responsible for the transportation of perishable cargo, and another division that transported general commodities, mainly textiles.

The company headquarters and the perishables division were moved to Lakeland, FL, in 1966 occupying a couple of small buildings in the corner of an orange grove. The general commodities division was established in Greenville, SC., in close proximity to then major textile lanes or routes.

In 1972, the company obtained its less-than-truckload (LTL) authority and that year became the first carrier to receive ICC authority to transport general commodities between California and Florida. The next year, Watkins became the first carrier to operate long-haul teams (two drivers alternating driving and rest periods) between Florida and California and more specifically between Los Angels and Miami in four days.

Shortly after expanding its transcontinental network in the late 1970s, Watkins improved the efficiency of its freight operations and billing functions by beginning on-line billing to its customers and establishing centralized rating, dispatching, tracing and customer coding.

During the mid 70s, BW hired Ms. Irene Sutton, to begin what eventually became the first employee relations program in the company. The company had grown to a size where BW wasn't comfortable he still had an accurate, objective and unfiltered pulse and reading on the feelings of the employees and contractors. He engaged Ms. Sutton to travel to the terminals, visit with the employees and contractors and report back to him about what was going on, what the perceptions were of management, and how he might best address the shortcomings. Ms. Sutton continued in this roll until BW started the Employee Relations Department in the early 80s. To BW, nothing was more important than maintaining a positive and dedicated workforce, - a commitment that was handed down to his sons and in turn to his grandchildren.

In 1978 while the industry was bracing for major changes in the federal Motor Carrier Act, Watkins began to prepare to do business after deregulation. Watkins realized that accurate costing and pricing would give them a competitive edge in the "world after deregulation" where the shipping rates would no longer be fixed by the ICC, but would instead be subject to market pressures. The company began developing a data base that would analyze the cost of moving freight. The system cost more than $1 million to develop, but by 1984 when it was fully on-line, Watkins was far ahead of its competition in being able to accurately analyze profitability by customer, lane and shipment.

This was a radical change from the way trucking firms had been doing business, and W.B. (Buz) Watkins, BW's oldest son, then chairman of Watkins Motor Lines, said, "we had to look to marketing our services instead of simply operating our services....all truck lines have had to find more efficient ways to operate."

Along with getting a handle on costs, management also decided to expand its current customer base by offering a quality service package. This included not only good delivery service, but competitive rates and a freight management system.

Part of that package came in 1983 when Watkins began its customer dial-up service that gave customers up-to-the-minute information about a shipment's location, status and charges. This service was expanded further the next year when the automated pricing system went into effect. It allowed a customer to quickly look at a two-page table, then by cross referencing zip codes and weight class, the rate could be determined.

In 1984, the traditions of valuing each employee and contractor as an active participant in the Watkins work-family, and of giving the customer nothing less than the best, were passed on when BW appointed his sons, W.B. "Buz" Watkins as chairman and John Watkins as president of Watkins Motor Lines, Inc.

****

"We are a people business. We really think a lot of our people and we tie the total success of our operation to the people....We communicate with our people....to learn what is happening in the business from their viewpoint and to hear their ideas. It is important to communicate so that we are all pulling on the same rope. The success of the company depends on that communication." - Buz Watkins

BW remained active in the company's affairs and in those of its parent company, Watkins Associated Industries, until his death in 1998. He loved nothing more than attending the various company picnics that were held each year across the country where he could personally interact with the employees, contractors and their families. He never forgot the importance of maintaining that personal relationship. This deeply felt spirit and passion for open communications was ingrained not only in Buz and John, but also in all levels of the organization - it was, simply put, a religion of sorts.

In late 1989, Rose Ann Froberg interviewed John Watkins for an article in the company magazine where he shared his thoughts, his philosophy and his expectations for the years ahead. I believe these comments reflect the keys to the company's success over its 74-year history.

****

"In a way, the company is your home. I think about it that way and I hope everybody else does. Let's face it, for the next 20 years, or for however long you're going to work here, Watkins is your work home and if we all don't take care of it - each one of us - it won't be anybody's home." - John Watkins

"I want us to be careful that we keep doing what we said we were going to do and that we keep an eye on our target of being a 'niche carrier' which for us is service. It's going to take a lot of dedication so that we're not talked into trying to be all things to all people. I don't see us having 650 terminals like some other companies and I don't see us serving every nook and cranny in town - I see us as an LTL (less than truckload) long haul carrier that gives the best service around." - John Watkins

He went on, "We don't want to paint our trucks a different color just so the dirt won't show. We want to keep them white - we want people to see us. We just redesigned the "Flying W" on the trucks' air shields to be 36 inches instead of the present 24 inches just so people will see us coming down the road. We'll also build some more big terminals. Nobody is going to miss seeing us."

"I don't want us to ever lose sight of our target, and that target is giving the best premium LTL service in the industry. We want people to know we're proud of who we are. We've always been a little bit better than the other guys - our people are better - our service is a little bit better - our trucks are a little bit cleaner - we're a little bit tougher - and the sense of family that we have with our employees is a little bit stronger. It's that tradition - that sense of knowing the importance of working together to deliver that service to our customers that's allowed us to succeed." - John Watkins

The sense of family was always an integral part of the Watkins work ethic, and how to nurture that feeling as the company grew was as much of a challenge as achieving any business goal. John placed a high priority on hiring the right managers. He stated, "In trucking it's particularly hard to find a truly people-oriented person for managerial and supervisory position because many come from a union background where that's not a prime consideration. We're a union-free carrier, and we'll remain that way because we treat our people like people. Our open door policy guarantees that and I won't abide by anyone violating it."

"We want this to continue to be a good place to work - a place where our people feel comfortable with what they're doing, and with their management - we want the family feeling to continue. If we hire the right kind of managers, as well as other key people who understand and believe in our philosophy, and we hire the type of people who want to work in that kind of atmosphere, it can be done. Those people are out there and we're willing to leave positions open until we find them. All of our people are that important to us!"

****

"Start with good people, lay out the rules, communicate with your employees, motivate them and reward them. If you do all those things effectively, you can't miss." - Lee Iacocca - Chairman of Chrysler Corporation

During its 40 years of growth in Lakeland, Watkins was always a good corporate citizen as well. Its presence in the orange grove had grown to four buildings housing administrative offices and staff, plus a large terminal and regional maintenance shop, all facing Griffin Road, near Interstate 4 in North Lakeland.

Like many small towns, Lakeland's downtown area was eventually abandoned by its original department stores when a large retail mall was built near the interstate. To stem the tide of gentrification that had eventually taken place, the downtown development council reached an agreement with Watkins to renovate and occupy a vacant former department store in exchange for a long term lease, right to purchase, and some initial tax incentives.

The Watkins organization invested over $4 million in the old Burdines Department Store one block from Main Street on East Lemon Street in downtown Lakeland, eventually relocating several of its largest departments like Accounting and IT to the newly renovated and highly functional building. With almost 500 employees working out of the new building, along with another company occupying a vacant property, the combined workforces needed places to eat and shop. The downtown center was again vital and flourishing. In addition to this major investment in the town of Lakeland, Watkins also made significant contributions to an assortment of local charities and the annual United Way fund drive.

At this point, the history of Watkins Motor Lines has been outlined in sufficient detail to give you an appreciation for the company's core values and to understand what a unique organization it was within the transportation industry. Now begins my journey and some of the many insights and lessons that I learned during my tenure with Watkins. I joined the company in May 1991 as Vice President of Human Resources after a long interview process. I almost didn't initially interview with them as they began a search for someone to head up the Human Resources function to help guide them on their aggressive expansion process across the country. Having spent years in the retail industry, I didn't believe that the trucking industry could be any more stable than the ever changing world of retail. However, upon my wife's urging, I met one morning in a joint interview with both Buz and John Watkins. The time just vanished as we talked about our backgrounds, the history of the company, and compared philosophies on a number of topics including their commitment to remaining union free and what I might offer the company in that regard. Before we all realized it, it was noon! I have never in my career had a three hour initial interview. What topped it off for me was John Watkins taking me on a tour of the complex before walking me to the door and shaking my hand as he promised to get back with me soon. Wow! Three hours plus a tour and it seemed like only 30 mins. They were so humble, so gracious, so giving of information, so comfortable, so honest, so real. We simply connected on many key issues - the chemistry was superb. I got in my car and pinched myself.

I have told people through the years, **"... the interview process is the best measure or litmus test of a prospective employer..."** Often it is, and should always be, their best foot forward. That is their time to market their corporate culture and values to a prospective employee. Think back to your last interview process. How were you treated leading up to and including the first interview? How was your first phone interview? How well were the travel and hotel arrangements made? Who greeted you upon arrival? Did the interviewer take interruptions during your interview? Did they make you feel like you were the most important thing on their schedule?

I was hooked after the first three hours at Watkins, but the total process took several more months of being interviewed and attending various dinners with staff officers and then weeks of hearing nothing in between those meetings. I almost gave up and told the headhunter that they obviously don't know what they were looking for and let us move on. He assured me that the process at Watkins was like that, a true courtship of sorts.

****

"Our employees are like extended members of our family." - Henry Ford - founder of Ford Motor Company.

Finally, my wife and I were invited to Lakeland, FL for a dinner with John Watkins and his wife and his other brother George. The dinner, as John told us, was an opportunity for them to tell my wife how important they felt the position of vp of Human Resources was to the company and that the process was so long in coming because they considered hiring an officer was like adding a member to their family. You guessed it - my wife was also hooked, because no organization in either of our careers took the time to make the spouse feel that he or she was an important part of the employment process. **Remember this - you are not hiring just an employee, you are hiring their family and loved ones into your organizational family. Make them all feel proud that their loved one is joining your organization.**

So, several weeks later, almost three months after my first interview, John extended the invitation to join Watkins Motor Lines. What I had learned about the Watkins family and their company during the interview process was exactly what became a reality upon joining the company. The Watkins family treated each employee with genuine dignity and respect, and everyone was made to feel like they indeed were part of a large friendly family unit.

The values I sensed and experienced from John and Buz during the interview process were the very values they incorporated into the fabric of the company's day to day operations and into their own personal lives. What you consistently got with a Watkins family member was humility, honesty, trustworthiness, integrity, and sincerity.

I have always believed that **a company cannot expect employees to be loyal to the organization if the senior leadership is not loyal to the employees.** In short, **loyalty down earns loyalty up.** Bill Watkins started that tradition in 1932 and the Watkins family continued to live it day in and out. The result was an unfailing trust between the workforce and management at all levels. If management said it, then employees knew it was true. Integrity was truly the base value that drove everything in the company - employee and contractor relations, customer relations, pricing, accounting standards, etc. What a unique environment it was - the expectation that everyone simply had to be honest in their day-to-day dealings with each other. Totally refreshing at first, then simply a routine expectation - a way of life.

****

"The supreme quality for leadership is unquestionably integrity. Without it, no real success is possible, no matter whether it is on a section gang, a football field, in an Army, or in an office." - Dwight D. Eisenhower - thirty-fourth President of the United States

During the growth years everyone in management invested countless hours in the recruiting process to ensure that we hired nothing but a quality workforce. We incorporated various screening processes, testing instruments, extensive criminal and background checks, not to mention the hours of interviewing required for each level of employee hired. Nothing was more important than to hire right the first time; and during that time I kept my message simple: **"Don't hire SLUGS!"** To short cut the hiring process and hire a "slow moving, lethargic, unproductive ground crawler" only results in a problem the manager will have to deal with down the road. Yes, companies do hire their problems; and if by chance you do hire a SLUG, get rid of it as soon as you recognize your mistake. Slugs bring a company down a slippery slope that affects service levels and product lines. **Don't shortchange the hiring process.**

****

"Endeavors succeed or fail because of the people involved. Only by attracting the best people will you accomplish great deeds." - Colin Powell - Chairman of Joints Chiefs of Staff and Secretary of State

In my opinion, to understand a major key to the success of Watkins growth, is to understand their business model at the terminal level. Each terminal was a separate operating business. The Watkins family believed that a strong entrepreneurial philosophy in each terminal drove the overall success of the whole company. Each terminal manager had their own profit & loss responsibility, their own sales staff, their own customer base, etc. In essence, they operated the terminal as if it was their own business. Each year, each terminal's sales and operating goals were established; as well as bonus payout levels for the account executives and terminal management. Everything that happened throughout the year was accounted for in the terminal's financial statement - equipment repairs, facility maintenance, customer entertainment, freight damage claims, electricity, fuel costs, etc. The sales bonus was earned and paid out each month while operating bonus payouts were earned and paid each quarter. The bonus payout potential was significant, which helped the company attract and keep the best talent in the industry. As I learned quickly, holding a manager totally accountable for the success of his or her respective business unit and then rolling it all up to a regional and then a corporate goal was a winning formula.

What was also amazing to me was that this was a privately-held company, but there were no secrets about who had what goals or who achieved their sales quotas or who earned their bonus rewards. I have not been with many publicly-traded companies that openly shared the financial information of the operation with its workforce the way a privately held company like Watkins Motor Lines did. **Give each manager total responsibility for his or her business unit, and reward performance with recognition and compensation and you have a fully committed workforce with everyone pulling in the same direction.**

****

"In Picking People: Look for intelligence and judgement and most critically, a capacity to anticipate, to see around corners. Also look for loyalty, integrity, a high-energy drive, a balanced ego, and the drive to get things done." - Colin Powell

From 1991 through 2000, working from a deliberate plan to fill in customer service gaps across the country, the company grew from 72 terminals to 133. Although growing rapidly, the company continued to place heavy emphasis on open communications and recognition. Everyone in management was intimately familiar with our HR mantra: **"The cornerstone of an effective Employee Relations Program is communications!"** And the company devoted significant time, money and resources to ensure that every employee felt they could openly communicate with all levels of the organization and that their efforts would be recognized. At Watkins, communication and recognition were not just lip service, but an integral part of the fabric of the culture. To that end, some of the communications and recognition programs included:

- The Open Door Policy which guaranteed each employee the opportunity to discuss a work-related problem with management.
- Regularly scheduled Round Table meetings at each location that promoted two-way, question-and-answer interaction.
- The Speak Up! program, which was a form an employee could fill out with a question, complaint, idea, whatever and send it directly to the company president. If the form was signed, the employee was guaranteed a timely response.
- A dedicated telephone Employee Hot Line to the company president where the caller was guaranteed confidentiality.
- The Rolex Club for any full-time employee or contractor who obtained 20 years of unbroken service with the company. The person being recognized was awarded a Rolex watch, typically by the company president, and was the guest of honor at a gathering of fellow employees and family members. These were very moving testimonies to the value of loyalty, friendship, hard work and to the true meaning of workplace family.
- Birthday and Service Anniversary cards were personally signed by the company president and sent to each employee on their birthday and their service anniversary every year. Artists created new designs for the cards each year, which became keepsakes for many employees.
- Safe driving awards began with the completion of a driver's first year and could culminate with the driver being awarded a $10,000 check, plus a personalized, custom tractor for his

own use, when he completed 25 years of driving without a preventable accident.
- Company wide Employee Opinion Surveys were also scheduled periodically to gauge sentiment about the company's benefits, working conditions and management.
- A number of company publications and bulletins imparted operational and sales news and noted employee accomplishments on a regular basis.

Along with all of the communications and recognition programs there were also the annual company picnics, which dated back to the beginning of the company. They were held at each location for employees, contractors and their families. Senior management would divide up the picnic schedule and spend the summer months traveling from coast-to-coast to maintain that face-to-face contact and listen to the heartbeat of the organization – its employees and its contractors.

Although not a communication or recognition program per se, one Watkins tradition that certainly bolstered the workplace family feeling was its policy of free coffee, tea and hot chocolate for everyone 24/7. There was no such thing as having to look for a cup of coffee, tea or hot chocolate – the pots were bottomless. A lot of time was spent chatting and talking about the business around the coffee stations. It seemed that nothing reinforced open communications better than time spent sharing freshly brewed coffee in a trusting environment.

Looking toward the year 2000, John saw a company solidifying its sales territories; expanding into New England and some additional states in the Midwest, and aiming at $1 billion a year in revenue. He passionately believed that, while the company may look different over time, philosophically it would remain the same.

In 2003, Buz's son, Chip, succeeded John Watkins as president, and John's son, Clay, became the executive vice president of Operations. John assumed the chairman of the board and CEO position, while Buz became board vice chairman. Both Chip and Clay came to their positions the same way their fathers had - by working their way up through the many hourly and management positions that the company had to offer. Again, the family culture instilled by BW was that everyone in key leadership positions had to earn his way up the ladder, not have it bestowed upon him as a birth right.

In 2004, Watkins Regional Express was established and the company entered the one-and two-day freight market. Regional, or "next day" hubs were opened in six cities and proved to be very successful. Nationwide expansion plans were made to extend the regional hub business from coast to coast. At that time this was totally unprecedented in the trucking industry. A company was either a "long haul" carrier such as Watkins Motor Lines with very long lengths of haul, or they were a regional "next day" carrier with short lengths of haul. For a company to do both out of the same terminal network was unheard of.

Also in 2004, the holding company, Watkins Associated Industries purchased Fairway Canadian Express and began operating as Watkins Canada Express. These two new ventures kept everyone looking forward and continuing to grow the business. To everyone at Watkins, the good times were on a roll.

****

"Outstanding leaders go out of their way to boost the self-esteem of their personnel. If people believe in themselves, it is amazing what they can accomplish." - Sam Walton - founder of Walmart and Sam's Club

In 2005, only the Watkins family knew that the FedEx Corporation had approached the family for the second time in a year to consider being acquired. Although a difficult decision, the timing turned out to be perfect for both parties, and in May of 2006, FedEx announced it had bought the business assets of Watkins Motor Lines and Watkins Canada Express for approximately $780 million cash. The sale was finalized in September of that year, and with that transaction, the company that had started out with one driver and one truck in 1932, and had over the years, grown to be the seventh largest LTL company in the United States and Canada with more than $1 billion revenue and more than 10,000 employees and contractors in 139 locations - ceased to exist in name, and unknowingly, as you will read in subsequent chapters, also in substance.

****

"The final test of a leader is that he leaves behind him in other men the conviction and the will to carry on." - Walter Lippman - American writer, political commentator, and Pulitzer Prize winner

MY CHAPTER 2 - LEADERSHIP "AHA'S"

****

- Study the complete history of your organization to gain appreciation for its hard won battles, how it evolved, what it stands for, and to understand its, all important, work culture.
- Don't shortchange the hiring process.
- Don't hire SLUGS!
- The interview experience for a prospective employee should be memorable since you only have one chance to make a good first impression.
- When you hire an employee remember that you are also hiring their family into your organizational family.
- Loyalty down earns loyalty up.
- Celebrate organizational and employee milestones, just the same as you do with your family - birthdays, anniversaries, promotions, a good report card, a team victory, etc.
- Always remember - "The Cornerstone of an effective Employee Relations Program is Communication."
- "The supreme quality for leadership is unquestionably integrity."
- You cannot devote enough hours to boosting the self-esteem of your employees.
- The more responsibility you give a manager, the more commitment that manager will give to the organization.

WHAT ARE YOUR CHAPTER 2 - "AHA'S?"

- _____
- _____
- _____
- _____

WHAT IS YOUR FAVORITE QUOTE?

- _____

Chapter 3

THE EVOLUTION OF FEDEX FREIGHT

****

"The life of an entrepreneur is occasionally exhilarating, and almost always exhausting. Only unbridled passion for the concept is likely to see you through the 17-hour days (month after month) and the painful mistakes that are part and parcel of the startup process." - Tom Peters - *American writer on business practices*

To understand the evolution of FedEx Freight is to first review the early history of the FedEx Corporation and its subsequent acquisitions. Just type in "FedEx" on your favorite search engine and many sites will pop up with the story of how founder, Frederick W. Smith, started the company in 1971 and began operations in 1973 as Federal Express. His business goal was to create a company that could provide an efficient nationwide express package delivery system. Unquestionably, FedEx revolutionized the way that package delivery was thought of in the business world. It replaced the model of using the same routes as passenger airlines and developed economically feasible systems and methods of guaranteeing overnight package delivery throughout the nation and eventually worldwide. FedEx was the first company in American history to reach $1 billion in less than 10 years without a merger or takeover.

Today, FedEx operates in hundreds of countries providing next-day service to millions of customers. It has set the benchmark for reliability and speed, and is without a doubt, one of the world's most recognized and respected brands.

FedEx Corporation oversees eight different operating companies that include: FedEx Express, FedEx Ground, FedEx Office, FedEx Trade Networks, FedEx Supply Chain Solutions, FedEx Services and FedEx Freight. These companies have their own separate management structures, provide services to customers unique to their specific markets and function under the motto of "operate independently, compete collectively and manage collaboratively." They have long held the belief that by operating independently, each company can focus exclusively on delivering the best service for its specific market while competing collectively ensures that all the companies benefit from their world wide brand.

All of the operating companies are expected to function under the same people-oriented work culture of "People-Service-Profit" or PSP. This is based on the philosophy that taking care of their people will lead them to deliver great service to their customers, who will in turn contribute to business profitability. This principle is further reinforced with the worldwide mantra for the FedEx workforce to fulfill the "Purple Promise" which is a collective commitment to "make every FedEx experience outstanding."

VIKING FREIGHT BECOMES THE FOUNDATION OF FEDEX FREIGHT

The story of FedEx Freight started in 1998 when Federal Express acquired Caliber Systems for approximately $2.4 billion from Roadway Express. Caliber was comprised of several different types of transportation companies, one of which was Viking Freight – a company with a very similar history and culture to Watkins Motor Lines.

Viking was started in 1966 in Santa Clara, CA, by a young man named Dick Bangham with $600 cash, a station wagon and an old pickup truck. During the 1970s they added more customers, equipment and people. During the 1980s Dick's younger brother,

Randy Bangham took the helm as president and accelerated its growth from a California intrastate carrier to an interstate regional carrier. During the 1990s Viking continued to gain market share and became the West's leading LTL transportation provider serving customers in the one- and two-day regional markets.

Dick Bangham created a very loyal non-union workforce as he fostered trust, commitment and longevity. The company had many awards programs for length of service, safe working and safe driving. They also had barbecues to commemorate team accomplishments; and each service center break room was equipped with a pool table, ice maker and a variety of vending machines. The senior leadership was dedicated to extensive communications programs through employee meetings, newsletters, informational videos and audiotape programs.

In 1988, Roadway Express, Inc. acquired Viking Freight. Over the next seven years, through a series of acquisitions and reorganizations, Viking became part of a regional transportation group that served over 90% of the U.S. population. This transportation group, under the Roadway umbrella, eventually became known as Caliber Systems, Inc. In 1997, dissatisfied with operating results, Roadway shut down two of the regional carriers within the group and sold the third to an investment group. In 1998, FedEx purchased Caliber and Viking Freight became the foundation for FedEx Freight.

Under FedEx, Viking Freight continued to operate in 11 Western states as a regional provider of premium one- and two-day service. The company also continued to foster its rich culture and its commitment to its 5,400 employees. Its partnership with FedEx was indeed a good one.

****

"Company cultures are like country cultures. Never try to change one. Try, instead, to work with what you've got." - Peter Drucker - *management consultant, educator, and author*

FEDEX ACQUIRES AMERICAN FREIGHTWAYS

In November 2000, the FedEx Corporation announced its agreement to acquire American Freightways Corporation for approximately $1.2 billion. As stated in its press release, the acquisition would allow FedEx Corp to extend its reach by expanding its reliable, next-day regional less-than-truckload (LTL) freight service with all points coverage in 48 states. The joint revenues of American Freightways and Viking would create the second-largest regional LTL freight unit in the United States.

****

"This acquisition is a perfect strategic fit that will give FedEx a unique competitive advantage, generating incremental volume and revenue that neither business could capture as a stand-alone." - Frederick W. Smith - founder of FedEx Corporation

American Freightways, based in Harrison, Arkansas, was founded in 1982 by Sheridan Garrison and was originally titled Arkansas Freightways. The company went through incredible growth and expanded rapidly in the regional one-day and two-day freight market. In 1989, it became a publicly-held corporation, and continued to aggressively develop a wide network of customer service centers providing direct shipping to 40 states. The company officially changed its name to American Freightways in 1993.

Like Viking, American Freightways developed a genuine commitment to building and maintaining a highly energized and loyal workforce. They routinely held a variety of employee communications meetings, held family picnics and recognition events and programs, distributed various targeted newsletters, video and audio programs for designated employee groups, celebrated victories, accomplishments, etc. From its founding day to the FedEx announcement, the company was lead by the founder and his selected senior leadership team. There was deep respect held for Sheridan Garrison and immense pride in the company. Employees trusted senior management and trusted whatever decisions were made, ultimately by Sheridan himself. His announcement of the FedEx acquisition and his taking a position on the Board of Directors of the FedEx Corporation solidified to his workforce that the partnership with FedEx was indeed, a very good thing.

****

"For American Freightways, joining forces with FedEx is a win-win situation for our shareholders, customers, and employees." - Sheridan Garrison - founder of American Freightways

American Freightways' 17,000 employees continued to operate in a business-as-usual manner following the acquisition and worked collaboratively with Viking in meeting customer expectations seamlessly from coast to coast.

****

"These two networks complement each other geographically, matching Viking's leadership in the West with American Freightways' strong presence throughout the Midwest, South and Northeast. We believe this business model offers superior benefits, without the inherent trade-offs of a one-size-fits-all approach."
Frederick W. Smith - *founder of FedEx Corporation*

FEDEX FREIGHT IS FORMED

In 2001, FedEx Corporation announced it would establish a FedEx Freight operating company to provide broad oversight to both American Freightways and Viking Freight. The newly established "holding company" was based in Memphis, TN. In 2002, it renamed Viking Freight - FedEx Freight West, and American Freightways - FedEx Freight East - both operating under the common name of FedEx Freight. Thus, a new operating segment of FedEx Corporation was created.

FEDEX ACQUIRES WATKINS MOTOR LINES' ASSETS

In May 2006, FedEx Corporation announced the acquisition of the assets of privately-held Watkins Motor Lines, Inc., including Watkins Canada Express. The announcement stated that FedEx Freight and Watkins had complementary service offerings. The addition of Watkins' three-day or more long-haul service to FedEx Freights industry-leading next-day and second-day regional LTL service was intended to extend FedEx's leadership position in the freight sector. The acquisition was completed in September 2006, and Watkins Motor Lines was rebranded FedEx National LTL, while Watkins Canada Express became FedEx Freight Canada. Both were to operate under the FedEx Freight segment of the FedEx umbrella.

****

"This acquisition will extend our leadership position in the heavy freight sector and provide new growth opportunities for the business." - Frederick W. Smith - *founder of FedEx Corporation*

As was stated many times, this relatively new organization within the FedEx enterprise was set up to "operate independently while competing collectively and managing collaboratively." Its structure however, resulted in very complicated lines of authority, communications, benefit structures, pay and bonus plans, and operating policies and procedures. In 2006, the FedEx Freight holding company, based in Memphis, provided oversight to FedEx Freight West, FedEx Freight East, FedEx National LTL and FedEx Freight Canada. However, the holding company had its own president and staff to provide guidance, while each of the "field companies" also had their own president and operational staff. FedEx Freight West was based in San Jose, CA, FedEx Freight East was in Harrison, AR, FedEx National was headquartered in Lakeland, FL, and FedEx Freight Canada was in Toronto.

In addition to its own management staff, the holding company and each of the "field companies" also had their own personnel and operational policies. To say "turf protection" hampered attempts to standardize policies and procedures across the entire organizational platform is an understatement. As of this writing, all of that confusion and complication has been resolved. This book is about the tumultuous journey everyone within the FedEx Freight segment endured and the impact it had on the 10,000 employees that were Watkins Motor Lines/FedEx National LTL.

Now, the story of that journey begins.

****

"For many men, the acquisition of wealth does not end their troubles, it only changes them." - Lucius Annaeus Seneca - Roman philosopher

MY CHAPTER 3 - LEADERSHIP "AHA'S"

****

- Acquisitions are enormous undertakings that require extensive planning and impeccable execution.
- Acquisitions affect not only the employees belonging to the acquired organization, but the employees of the acquiring organization, as well as, the customers loyal to both organizations.
- Acquisitions are very exciting times, but also are laced with anxiety and fear of the unknown for all interested stakeholders - the stock holders, the employees, and the customers.
- You can never over-communicate during an acquisition, but it is critical that all communications are straightforward and provide as much relevant detail as possible.
- Recognize and respect the impact on the converging company cultures.

WHAT ARE YOUR CHAPTER 3 - "AHA'S?"

- _____
- _____
- _____
- _____

WHAT IS YOUR FAVORITE QUOTE?

- _____

And You Call This F-ing Leadership?

Chapter 4

THE ASSET ACQUISITION

****

"Obviously, despite hard work and heroic efforts, many dreams don't come true. But, if we don't dare to dream and then throw muscle, heart, and soul into making the dreams come true, then WOW Projects - - and all of the emotional, intellectual, spiritual, and financial riches that they bring - - will surely NOT be our lot in life." - Tom Peters - *American writer on business practices*

The acquisition process for me started in August of 2005 when John Watkins called me into his office and before we started to talk he handed me a Non-Disclosure Agreement to sign. It stated that if I talked to anyone about this project outside those authorized, I would be terminated and possibly prosecuted. WOW! That got my attention! After I signed it, he sat back and told me that other than Watkins family members and the Board of Watkins Associated Industries, only our executive vice president of Operations, our vice president Controller, and I would be involved. We would be working on due diligence assignments through outside attorneys hired to assist the family in selling the company to the FedEx Corporation. Nothing could have surprised me more than if he had loaded one of his prized collector Browning shotguns and aimed it at me.

Once I recovered from my initial shock, John gave me the details of how the family had been approached by the president of FedEx Freight over a two year period and how the last offer was finally accepted. The "why" of the decision was never truly explained; and in reality, it doesn't much matter at this point. My personal opinion is that the offer was simply too compelling to ignore. As John had said for all the years I knew him, "Cash is King." Sweet and simple. My job now was to facilitate that transaction.

****

"The world hates change, yet it is the only thing that has brought progress."
Charles Kettering - inventor and founder of Dayton Engineering Laboratories Company (Delco)

The one thing I did understand after my meeting, however, was that the family couldn't think of a better company than FedEx to acquire Watkins. FedEx was, and still is, one of the most admired companies in the world, with a reputation of superior customer service and taking care of its employees. That was key for John – taking care of the employees. This, he felt, made the proposition from FedEx not only good financially for the Watkins family, but also good for the Watkins employees and their families.

During the next several months, the three of us on the transaction team secretly pulled reports, gathered massive amounts of information and worked through what seemed like endless meetings with the attorneys to provide FedEx with whatever was requested. Shortly after the Christmas holidays, the family got permission to bring the rest of our officers in on the project due to the amount of information requested from virtually all departments. This group also had to sign the Non-Disclosure Agreements. Rumors were already beginning to churn. To have our entire officer team on board made it much easier to delay certain operating decisions, stall commitments on longer range purchases, delay hiring for key positions, etc.

By early spring, rumors of a sale were getting almost unbearable to manage. Remember, we were an organization based on honesty and trust. We didn't deceive our employees. But nor were they unintelligent automatons! These were intelligent, thinking people being asked for unusual data. Now there was a great deal going on that couldn't be explained, or if explanations were given, they often rang hollow. Outside appraisers were also beginning to show up at terminals trying to discretely take pictures. We were being questioned on why simple contracts or purchases were being delayed. The more questions were left unanswered or answered poorly, the more rampant the rumors became. A foreboding shadow began to hang over our day-to-day operations as we attempted to work under the guise of business-as-usual.

Throughout my career, I have been intrigued by why some companies announce to their workforce that they are in talks with another company about merging, being bought or sold; while others work hard to keep it confidential and secret from their employees. Realistically, there is probably no right or wrong approach. However, as I look back on my personal experiences, I can definitely say that the price paid for secret and confidential projects is way too often paid primarily by the employees. The very foundation of trust and confidence in management is eroded once employees realize that they are the victims and not the partners in the change taking place. Too often trust cannot be rebuilt.

****

"Trust is the lubrication that makes it possible for organizations to work."
Warren G. Bennis - American scholar, organizational consultant and author

As our staff went through this due diligence process it became clear that because this was to be an asset purchase, once the official announcement was made, we would have to transition our equipment titles, registrations, employee records over to FedEx and that that process would have to be handled by FedEx Freight employees and not us. So, once all the information had been shared and the presentations made, there was little for us to do but wait until the official announcement, which was scheduled for around Memorial Day weekend of 2006.

As with all the best laid plans, one week before the planned announcement, one of the local newspapers in Memphis, The Commercial Appeal, ran a story about the acquisition of Watkins Motor Lines, even including the secret code name for the project – Convoy. All of our Memphis based employees had the story before the rest of the country woke up, and it spread like wild fire through the trucking grapevine. All the details of the purchase were there in black and white. Our employees were shocked and numb, but because it was not an official announcement FedEx declined to comment and we couldn't say anything, so the story just hung there in the air — for an entire week. We simply had to wait until FedEx made it official. It was later discovered the leak had come from the FedEx side, but finding the source made no difference, the damage had already been done.

****

"The void created by the failure to communicate is soon filled with poison, drivel, and misrepresentation." - C. Northcote Parkinson - British Naval historian and author

The official announcement was finally made on Friday, May 26, 2006 - Memorial Day Weekend. While no real surprise at this point, the workforce was still shocked with the reality that the Watkins family would actually sell the company and that some of the rumors and speculation ended up being true. Some compared it to finding out your parents had put you up for adoption. Remember, many of our employees had spent their entire career working for the Watkins family and they now faced, what was to them, a very uncertain future. Shock and disbelief is an understatement. Even some of the Watkins family members were not happy with the reality; but, as most people do, they shifted into survival mode and began feeling cautiously optimistic about their new parent - the world famous FedEx Corporation. Indeed, our employees experienced a host of mixed emotions.

In the announcement, our employees were informed that Chip Watkins would be serving as president of the new FedEx Freight subsidiary and reporting to the FedEx Freight EVP and COO. Clay Watkins would also be transitioning to the new company as senior vice president of Operations Support. Two Watkins family members moving with the workforce - indeed an optimistic message during a time of extreme anxiety and unknown.

On the day of the announcement, a plane load of FedEx Freight senior executives flew to Lakeland to hold a large group meeting with our Lakeland-based management team and to hold a conference call with our field management. Their goal was to assure everyone that nothing was going to change and that this was going to be a perfect relationship for both FedEx Freight and our employees. We would have the new name of FedEx National LTL and would continue to provide our long haul LTL service as a complement to the FedEx Freight East and West regional one-day and two-day service lanes. This acquisition was truly a growth strategy for the Freight segment of FedEx. It is an understatement to say the day was the culmination of roller coaster emotions for everyone over the previous several months.

****

"FedEx changed the landscape in the freight industry by delivering time-sensitive LTL shipments with the reliability for which FedEx is known. This acquisition is an opportunity to do more business with our current shippers and to target new customers with a comprehensive LTL solution - allowing us to grow faster than the industry in which we operate." - Douglas G. Duncan - President and CEO of FedEx Freight Corporation

Immediately after the announcement, an 11-minute DVD entitled "Watkins Motor Lines to Join FedEx Freight" was distributed throughout the company. It was a "welcome to FedEx" conversation between the president and ceo of FedEx Freight and Chip Watkins - targeted to our employees. They discussed how FedEx National LTL would operate as the long haul service provider while FedEx Freight's regional networks would continue in the one-day and two-day service lanes. They stressed FedEx's desire to hire our independent pick-up and delivery contractors as employees since that was the model at FedEx Freight for customer facing positions. They also expressed the desire to make offers to purchase the contractors' equipment, which to all of us was a very significant gesture since some of our contractors had 20 or more years of working with Watkins. The president and CEO of FedEx Freight made it clear to all viewers that "The people side of this business is imperative."

****

"The older I get the less I listen to what people say and the more I look at what they do." - Andrew Carnegie - founder of Carnegie Steel Company (U.S.Steel)

At this point we knew our new name but not much about how we would transfer from Watkins as employees to FedEx as "assets." The closing of the acquisition was scheduled for the first week in September. In an asset purchase, the acquired assets move from the seller to the buyer upon closing. In this case, the seller (Watkins) continued to exist and retained the name Watkins Motor Lines, Inc. I have never been able to determine a concrete reason why the purchase was asset based, and at this point it doesn't really matter. As many of us often said to each other during this period and the years to follow; **"It is what it is."**

What shocked us was that, right after the announcement, no one at FedEx Freight Inc. headquarters in Memphis or Freight East in Harrison, AR, knew what procedures or processes would be used for moving our "asset" workforce from Watkins to FedEx, nor did they have it planned. *Really?* We also learned that the vp of Human Resources and the Human Resources Department at FedEx Freight East would be coordinating the, as yet unplanned, "hiring" process. We were told that legally, because this was an asset purchase, and we were assets, we could not hire ourselves. *Welcome to the family!*

****

"Plan your progress carefully; hour-by-hour, day-by-day, month-by-month. Organized activity and maintained enthusiasm are the wellsprings of your power." - Paul J. Meyer - author

After some long agonizing weeks, the plan finally began to take shape. Our entire workforce including any contractors who wished to become employees, would have to complete a FedEx National LTL application for employment. These would then be collected and turned over to the FedEx Freight HR office in Harrison. That group would then conduct background checks through an outside vendor. Then, everyone would be required to take a drug test. So far so good except they had no plan for the drug testing nor a vendor to handle the process. We ended up working with our own vendor who conducted our random testing for Watkins. The results were then fed to the FedEx Freight office in Harrison.

Eventually, if one passed the background check including not being on a "No Rehire" list from previous employment with a FedEx company before joining Watkins, passing the drug test, and completing the government Form I-9 (verifying immigration status), one of six different versions of an "offer letter of employment" could be issued. After our employees signed these letters they could then be authorized to transition over to the payroll of FedEx National LTL on the closing day. The offer letter contained the person's new job title, pay rate, among other information. Procedures also had to be developed for handling and processing the Watkins employees who were out on any form of a Leave of Absence, including military leave. Talk about a coordination nightmare.

Since the closing was targeted for the first part of September, we roughly had only 10 weeks to get this done for our entire workforce of almost 10,000 employees and contractors. This meant every headquarters manager or department head, every field terminal, shop, line haul and operations manager had to completely re-hire their entire staff, all at once. We all then needed to complete the benefit enrollment process and re-enroll all our employees in roughly our same benefits and vendors, but under a new contract coordinated this time out of the Freight East office with new forms to recognize the new company. All of this while we were continuing to run our normal day to day operations in the trucking business while trying to explain to customers what this change would mean to them.

****

"Organizing is what you do before you do something, so that when you do it, it is not all mixed up." - A. A. Milne - English author, playwright, and poet

For our field operations employees, most of the summer months were filled with terminal visits from FedEx Freight officers, Chip, Clay and our Watkins operations officer group. These meetings were face-to-face with our employees answering questions and attempting to make everyone feel welcome and comfortable with the uncertainty of the upcoming change of ownership. It goes without saying that this was a very stressful time for almost all the employees throughout the country. They were truly scared of the unknown and for some, they were grieving the loss of Watkins Motor Lines. I recall a manager telling me that these visits were like the preacher coming to tell everyone they were going to a better place. However, in my career, I don't think I have seen such a committed effort by an acquiring company to work with a large field workforce to try to ease anxieties and nervousness. They truly tried to deliver a meaningful message to our drivers, dockworkers, clerical, sales and field management staff.

****

"The ability to summon positive emotions during periods of intense stress lies at the heart of effective leadership." - Jim Loehr - *author and world renowned performance psychologist*

However, at our headquarters that 10-week period was probably the most stressful I've ever seen a workforce endure. My department worked seven day weeks, ate three catered meals a day in the office and got very little sleep in between. All vacations were cancelled and employees with children had to make alternate arrangements for evening child care. What complicated the process was that, in addition to working on transitioning all of our employees, we also had to operate as Watkins Motor Lines which meant continuing all of our normal HR procedures and practices in order to maintain our operation until the acquisition was finalized. I can only speak for the Watkins HR Department, but I can imagine the workload and stress levels were similar for the HR group in Harrison.

And the HR departments were not the only ones affected. All of the equipment licenses and registrations for thousands of tractors, trailers and company cars had to be converted, as well as all of the other assets including lease agreements, property and tax records, to mention only a few. The stress of that transition definitely took its toll on the enthusiasm and excitement of being acquired. Those most directly involved with the asset acquisition failed to feel any warmth from the FedEx welcome wagon; but despite it all, everyone was steadfastly committed to doing their very best so that Watkins would be seen as a "can do" group – and they did.

One amusing transition requirement that summer was that my HR director had to work full time for two weeks completing an exhaustive assessment and valuation questionnaire on our employee population. This was so the valuation vendor hired by FedEx Freight could determine the dollar value of our Human Resources as assets.

To my knowledge, no other company has been acquired in this manner by FedEx, at least for sure not in the FedEx Freight segment. To this day, I doubt few within FedEx can fully appreciate the demands and emotional stress that our asset based acquisition had on a large share of the workforce.

****

"We tend to meet any new situation by reorganizing, and a wonderful method it can be for creating the illusion of progress while producing inefficiency and demoralization." - Petronious - Roman courtier and author

As the transition process progressed, not everyone received an offer letter to go forward for a host of valid employment justifications - failed background checks and criminal convictions (some that may have occurred while employed with Watkins that would prevent them from being hired by FedEx), failed drug screens, no rehire classifications from previous FedEx employment, etc.

Also, not everyone was "hired" into FedEx National LTL at the same position level they held in Watkins. For example, our field vice president-region managers were not hired as officers, they were offered their same job, but as managing director-region operations. Their counterparts at Freight were officers. Our vp's of Performance Standards, Maintenance, Real Estate, and Pricing were hired as managing directors and a number of our Watkins directors were hired as senior managers. Our vp of Safety left at closing and was not replaced in FedEx National LTL.

Neither Viking nor American Freightways employees experienced any of this in their acquisition processes into FedEx. So, while the announcement process promised that everything would remain the same, it didn't end up being totally true for everyone. But, in the spirit of "Thank God I have a job," "Lets get this moving and see how it plays out," everyone worked hard to make the best of it. Some who didn't wish to transition over to FedEx elected to leave Watkins and they left the company on the closing date.

After a very grueling summer, the day of the closing finally came at 12:01a.m. on September 4, 2006. My department worked through that entire weekend as well as on Labor Day. The computer programs worked, converting those who were offered continued employment from Watkins to the new FedEx National LTL. For the most part there was a feeling of cautious excitement throughout the company - our employees in the field were now officially members of the FedEx Freight family and our headquarters staff could be very proud of the jobs they did to accomplish this nightmarish transfer of assets. The field workforce celebrated Labor Day on Monday and came to work to their new company on Tuesday morning.

That Friday, September 8, our new company FedEx National LTL held a huge Birthday Celebration across the country with Freight counterparts joining with our workforce to help welcome former Watkins employees to the FedEx family. These events were cook outs with balloons, cakes, punch, meet-eat-and-greet functions. In Lakeland, at the general offices, folks from the Memphis Freight HQ and from Freight East in Harrison attended. What good events these were because they reminded our employees of our old Watkins culture of joining together to celebrate good times.

After the celebration, a 14 minute DVD entitled "Special News Edition of the Dispatcher - Sept 8th Official Birthday" was distributed throughout FedEx National LTL to commemorate the event. A special message from Chip Watkins and his new boss reinforcing their excitement over the growth strategy of running a separate long haul network within the Freight segment. Our first week at FedEx exceeded everyone's expectations. This truly seemed to be a perfect fit for everyone involved. As Chip's boss stated in the DVD - "Have Faith in the Future." Indeed, at that time, we all did.

MY CHAPTER 4 - LEADERSHIP "AHA'S"

****

- Nothing stays the same forever - especially organizations. Ongoing organizational change is a reality in today's ever changing world.
- Accept and embrace change or be suffocated by it.
- All major projects deserve, require, and demand extensive planning and organizing BEFORE the project begins, not during the evolution of the action.
- A well thought out and executed plan ensures confidence, support and commitment from the workforce.
- Good leaders stand and work with their employees during the long hours and tough times of major projects, and offer encouragement, support, and comfort. They get out from behind their desks and are truly present and involved during the tough challenges and times.
- Never ever, let me repeat, never ever make promises to a workforce that cannot be guaranteed without any doubt. In today's ever changing world, a promise and guarantee is almost impossible.
- Broken promises destroy your integrity and once that is destroyed it cannot be regained - the workforce will simply never trust you again.
- When bewildered by what is occurring around you and nothing seems to make much sense - repeat to yourself this simple pacifier: "IT IS WHAT IT IS!"

WHAT ARE YOUR CHAPTER 4 - "AHA'S?"

- _____
- _____
- _____
- _____

WHAT IS YOUR FAVORITE QUOTE?

- _____
  _____
  _____

And You Call This F-ing Leadership?

And You Call This F-ing Leadership?

Chapter 5

THE AMERICAN FREIGHTWAYS BIAS

****

"The first thing successful leaders must do is carefully assess the political culture of his or her group, and understand how it affects the distribution of power resources that will be available and the costs of their use." - Joseph S. Nye, Jr. - American political scientist at Harvard University

This chapter is presented here in the chronology because it is important to understand this bias as you follow the ensuing four year story of FedEx National LTL. Recall from Chapter 3 that Viking was the first LTL company acquired by the FedEx Corporation in 1996. That was followed by American Freightways in 2000. These two acquisitions led to the formation of the FedEx Freight Corporation, based in Memphis. It was set up as a holding company with Viking (FedEx Freight West) and American (FedEx Freight East) operating as separate independent companies, each having their own president and support functions.

The president and chief operating officer for the newly created FedEx Freight Corporation came from Viking. He was promoted around February 2001 and relocated to Memphis to establish the new corporate offices. Three (Finance, Legal and Marketing) of the seven senior officers for the new holding company came from other FedEx segments in Memphis, while the remaining four senior officers came from American. Of the four who came from American only one (Marketing) transferred to the new corporate offices in Memphis, the others remained in Harrison and ran their respective FedEx Freight Corporation functions from there. Those included the executive vice president of Operations and COO, the senior vice president of Operations Planning & Engineering, and the vice president of Risk Management.

When you combined the disproportionate share of senior officers (one from Viking, three from other FedEx segments and four from American) with the geographic challenges created by not having all of the holding company's functions under one roof, the new FedEx Freight segment was very much a house divided both by geography and culture. The group in Harrison, the group in San Jose and the group in the Memphis were worlds apart in many ways. They differed in benefits and compensation policies and practices, operating philosophies, communication styles, and in their views on employee relations. These differences bread distrust and disdain for each other. When we joined the organization as FedEx National LTL, we only made that disconnect between the three (Harrison, Memphis and San Jose) more obvious.

The American Freightways bias was fostered largely by its shear size and larger contribution to FedEx Freight's profits. Because of this, the voice of their senior leaders carried a great deal more influence over the entire Freight segment, and with each passing year (2006-2010) of FXNL's story, that voice became more prominent throughout the segment. For example, the president of Freight West (Viking) left the company and was back filled by a Freight East (American Freightways) officer. When the president of FedEx National LTL retired, he was replaced by a Freight East (American Freightways) officer. When the new position of vice president of operations was created at FedEx National LTL by the Freight leadership, a move that we believed enabled them to place their own person on our staff, the position was filled by a Freight East (American Freightways) officer who relocated to our Lakeland offices.

Other key positions at FedEx National LTL (also referred to as FXNL) were also filled by Freight East people. The managing director of financial planning and analysis was filled two months after the acquisition by a person from Freight East (American Freightways) from Harrison who relocated to Lakeland. When we had a vacancy created by the retirement of a managing director of regional operations, it was filled by a person from Freight East (American Freightways). The subtle message was loud and clear throughout our organization that the only capable and qualified people to fill key management positions at FedEx National LTL were from FedEx Freight East (American Freightways).

****

"The level of trust in business relationships....is a greater determinant of success than anything else, including content excellence." - Charles H. Green - Australian Army Officer

As evidenced above, the operating climate and ultimately the work culture of the FedEx Freight Corporation segment were heavily influenced and dominated by the culture of FedEx Freight East (American Freightways). Simply put, if they wanted it, they generally got it. Their operating philosophy and culture permeated not only Harrison, but from our perspective from the very beginning, the Memphis Freight offices as well, or at least they heavily influenced the final decisions over the overall segment. The "Corporate" culture at FedEx, that we had heard so much about through the years, had little influence throughout the Freight segment.

****

"The moment there is suspicion about a person's motives, everything he does becomes tainted." - Mahatma Gandhi - Indian philosopher and political leader

Recall that, when Watkins was acquired, it was the Human Resources Department at Freight East in Harrison that oversaw the entire hiring process of the Watkins work force, not the staff at Freight West in San Jose. As a matter of fact, we had very little contact with our counterparts from Freight West. Almost everything related to our acquisition was overseen by staff based in Harrison. The employees of Freight East (American Freightways) naturally believed their policies, processes and methodologies were better than others. The group from the corporate office in Memphis, as far as we could tell in the beginning, had very little influence over our acquisition processes. The die was cast almost from the beginning -

the American Freightways group had the bias, called the shots, had the power, and in most cases the last word.

Soon after the acquisition, FedEx National LTL was directed to give up all of the Regional next day freight, $100 million a year in revenue, and its corresponding profit. This revenue had been developed over the previous five years as Watkins Motor Lines established a Regional one and two-day business segment to compliment its primary long haul business. That freight revenue and volume went to Freight East because that, as we were told, was their business model and they had the processes and systems and sales force to continue supporting it. We on the other hand, did NOT get any of the long haul freight revenue and volume that Freight East or West was handling even though that was supposed to be our business model and supposedly the primary reason FedEx purchased Watkins. We had the model to oversee long haul freight, but, none the less, Freight East retained their long-haul freight, including the revenue and profit it generated, AND took some of ours.

Another example, all be it a small one, of the American Freightways bias had to do with celebrating our 75th anniversary. Clearly, not a big deal in the scheme of everything else going on, but, an important recognition of our roots and rich company history. We were very proud of our history and wanted to celebrate this incredible milestone. When we approached the Communications group at the Freight Corporate office in Memphis for guidance on how to proceed within the FedEx culture, we were politely told no, we were no longer Watkins and we needed to simply move on as a part of FedEx. While obviously very disappointed, we moved on and did not celebrate the 75th anniversary. We had been acquired and Watkins was now in the past. We understood the rationale, but to this day I regret we did not fight harder to celebrate this special milestone.

I say this because several months after our company anniversary date had passed, the senior vp of Marketing from the Memphis office (formerly from American Freightways) came to our Lakeland offices for a Monday staff meeting. While there he handed out commemorative 25th Silver Anniversary models of American Freightways trucks to some of our staff. Freight East had held a grand celebration in Harrison and throughout their company for reaching their 25th anniversary. We were shocked and obviously highly upset. We complained to Memphis and very much wanted to know why Freight East could celebrate its 25th and we could not celebrate our 75th! Their response was almost as shocking as the event itself. They stated and I quote: "They didn't ask us." *Really?* They could do as they wanted and for trying to play within the lines, play by the rules, we were prohibited from celebrating 50 more years of being in existence than they were! What a huge wake up call for us! The American Freightways bias and arrogance was beginning to be rubbed in our faces. They were clearly, without question, operating on their own terms. Hard for us to embrace the FedEx motto of "managing collaboratively."

Another strong signal to us of their power base within the Freight segment was the new restrictions on the handling of charitable contributions in our home town of Lakeland, FL, population 90,000. The Watkins company had been a good corporate citizen for years and had traditionally matched employee contributions to the United Way by 50% on the dollar and contributed additionally to other various local charities in addition to assisting employees with disaster relief funds after earthquakes, tornadoes and hurricanes. When we were acquired, no funding for charitable contributions was included in our budget, so the week after closing I had to start responding to requests from local charities indicating that we no longer could contribute company funds to their charities. We were now a FedEx company and we could not contribute to our local charities! What really shocked me was when I discovered, through my counterparts at Freight East and West, that hundreds of thousands of dollars of company funds were disbursed by Freight East in their home town of Harrison, AR, population 12,000, and by Freight West in their home area of San Jose, CA.

After decades of contributing to the Lakeland area, we no longer had funds for any contributions and that cold reality did not change for the next four years. After about a year, the managers of many of the local charities simply gave up on FedEx and finally stopped asking me why a company like FedEx could not contribute on the local level. Freight East and West could, we could not. Yup, the words continued to ring - "nothing is going to change."

During the four years that FedEx National LTL was in existence, most of the system or operating changes that were driven by Freight leadership were aimed at bringing the total organization into closer alignment. This was a good thing and a direction that was imperative for the long-term success of the Freight operating segment. However, most of the changes were defaulted to those procedures and processes in place at Freight East - whether they were better or not. Size drove the decisions. If we at FXNL had a better computerized delivery tracking system (which we did), for example, it didn't matter because we were told that it was easier to change over a smaller organization than a larger one. The "best practices" or technically most up to date systems, or procedures simply didn't matter.

Many of our senior leadership team never got used to the level of arrogance held by so many of the senior leaders in the Harrison location we worked with, not only during the acquisition, but also the years that followed. Don't get me wrong, many of the managers and staff personnel there were very pleasant and cooperative to deal with, but there remained an overall persistent level of arrogance that was not conducive to team building. Since the corporate staff based in Harrison appeared to be essentially the nerve center, we at FXNL felt, in many respects, that we had been acquired by FedEx Freight East, not by the FedEx Corporation. The American Freightways group made no apologies for the position of influence and power they held throughout the organization.

****

"Build for your team a feeling of oneness, of dependence on one another and of strength to be derived by unity." - *Vince Lombardi - Head Coach of the Green Bay Packers professional football team*

As previously stated, during the first several years the operating environment was very complex. The Freight West group had processes and procedures that had been in place long before American Freightways was even created as a company, so obviously their leadership group was not going to change anything without staunch resistance. They simply ignored most pressures to change. We at National also had our long established methods and ways of operating and believed, naively as it ended up being, that we could and should operate "independently." This was what we were told and believed from day one. It was a core component of the overall fundamental operating philosophy of the entire FedEx Corporation -

"operate independently, compete collectively and manage collaboratively."

As any reasonable business person might suspect, decision making for the entire Freight segment was difficult and complex. We operated under a "house divided" between the Corporate offices in Memphis and Harrison, and three separate Presidents and related staff officers and support functions at National LTL (in Lakeland, FL), Freight East (in Harrison, AR), and Freight West (in San Jose, CA). Everyone seemed committed to maintaining and protecting their respective turfs. Most outsiders would quickly question our sanity - everyone appeared in charge, which effectively meant no one was in charge. This structure, simply put, is not efficient nor cost effective nor organizationally functional. The big question remained - who was running the show? At the end of the day - the American Freightways crowd had the size, profit base, the bias, the advantage, and the arrogance, and were effectively running the entire operation.

One can quickly ascertain that this type of operating environment breeds mistrust. Something that I have strongly believed throughout my career is the need for a common staff function to work in close proximity to each other. The core staff who are essentially in charge of an organization need face to face access to each other on a routine basis. **Working closely with each other regularly, if not daily, is essential to collaboration and even more important, in my opinion, to building TRUST, which is the very foundation of effective organizations.** Teams are built through time spent together - having hall discussions, face to face meetings versus conference calls, going to lunch with each other, gathering to celebrate anniversaries, birthdays, etc. Time spent together talking about the business and about personal lives helps build trust and trust is essential in maintaining healthy business relationships.

****

"Mergers, downsizing, and globalization have accelerated the pace of change in organizations, creating a crisis of trust that didn't exist a generation ago." - Robert F. Hurley - Fordham University

Having essentially four different general office staff functions with respective officer groups believing they are all empowered to operate their organizations independently, all under one primary operating segment, further breeds confusion, resentment, and miscommunication. I sum up the work environment during much of our time at FedEx National LTL with the FedEx Freight segment simply as - dysfunctional.

****

"Culture does not change because we desire to change it. Culture changes when the organization is transformed; the culture reflects the realities of people working together everyday." - Frances Hesselbein - *founder and president of Leader to Leader Institute*

MY CHAPTER 5 - LEADERSHIP "AHA'S

****

- The hard cold reality of success in any organization is to understand and respect both the work place culture and the political culture.
- Underestimating and disregarding the history of an organization leads to discontent and distrust.
- People working in organizations must have high levels of respect in each other at all levels - respect is the glue that holds it all together and enables it to function effectively. Lack of respect breeds mistrust. Lack of trust leads to dysfunction.
- "...culture reflects the realities of people working together everyday."
- The leadership of core staff units should work closely together to build ongoing trust in each other and with the group as a whole.
- A great leader must create, respect, and manage the culture of his/her organization.
- All organizations need just one boss and a shared set of common goals. A house divided accomplishes little but confusion and maneuvering for power.
- Quickly accept the realities of the power bases within an organization and develop ways to succeed and use that reality to your advantage.

WHAT ARE YOUR CHAPTER 5 - "AHA'S?"

- _____
- _____
- _____

WHAT IS YOUR FAVORITE QUOTE?

- _____

And You Call This F-ing Leadership?

Chapter 6

A VERY SHORT HONEYMOON

****

"Annual income twenty pounds, annual expenditure nineteen nineteen six, result happiness. Annual income twenty pounds, annual expenditure twenty pounds ought and six, result misery." - Charles Dickens - British novelist

The week following the acquisition closing on Labor Day, 2006, was filled with the excitement over becoming a part of the world class business icon - the FedEx Corporation. It was also a period filled with mixed emotions - saying farewell to an era of being a part of a privately-held family-owned business, while also needing to quickly learn how to embrace a publicly-traded stock corporation. **Nothing seems to charge the spirit of a work environment more than entering a period of rapid change with all of the excitement and anticipation that the changes are going to be positive.** Shouldn't that be the objective of any company acquiring another - to create that positive perception? Overall, that is how most of us felt that first week, even given the changes we already were beginning to see and experience.

Changes in Sales – Recall from Chapter 2 that at Watkins Motor Lines, the field sales representatives reported directly to their respective terminal managers. Upon becoming FedEx National LTL, the field sales force now reported to one of three Sales managing directors who reported to the Sales vice president, who in turn reported to FXNL president. This change also ushered in a different bonus structure for the sales force that did not turn out as a positive - more on that later. The National Accounts sales executives continued to report to their National Accounts vice president, however, he now reported to the senior vice president of Marketing, who was based at the FedEx Freight headquarters in Memphis.

****

"Change is the process by which the future invades our lives." - Alvin Toffler - US social commentator and author of Future Shock.

The FXNL field sales force sold only freight that ran in long haul lanes – essentially freight that took three or more days from pickup to delivery. FedEx Freight East and West also each had their own respective sales organizations, who in turn sold their respective regional one- and two-day freight lanes. Neither Freight East or Freight West operated in the same geographical locations; however, FXNL had many terminals in the same locations as East and West.

Because of this geographical overlap, for the first time, there were now two "Freight" sales representatives from the same umbrella organization (FedEx Freight) calling on customers, in many cases the same customers, selling two different forms of freight or length of haul transportation services. This quickly became confusing for the customers, especially since each service (long and short haul) had different pricing criteria. It was not unusual for a Freight East or West representative and a National sales representative to find themselves sitting together in a customer's lobby waiting for their separate appointments. Eventually, on their own initiatives, they started making appointments together which reduced, but did not eliminate some of the confusion and frustration for the customers.

****

"Customers do not care about industry boundaries; they want service and convenience." - Peter G. W. Keen - US information technology consultant

Think about it — two different sales representatives, each with different service offerings, each priced differently, each with different phone numbers for pickups and service issue follow-up — and if that wasn't enough to fuel confusion — each had its own bills of lading and invoices. No wonder there was confusion in the marketplace and friction within the sales forces. Many of the representatives perceived the other as infringing on their territories and competing for their customers' loyalty.

One might think that the split sales structure would have been thought through by the FedEx Freight leadership before, or at least during the acquisition process and a solution determined to reduce the impact of what became a growing negative customer experience in the months following the acquisition. But it wasn't. More on the eventual sales reorganization in later chapters.

****

"A man who does not think and plan long ahead will find trouble right at his door." - Confucius - Chinese teacher, editor and philosopher

Changes in Operations - Recall that all Watkins Motor Lines terminal managers had their own separate profit and loss statements and operated their units as a separate business along with very specific revenue and profit goals. They were responsible for and aware of the profit and loss of their sales accounts and of their own terminals. At FedEx Freight, the terminals or service centers, as they are called, do not have their own profit and loss statements.

As our managers began to adjust to this new operating model, they struggled with not having the financial information they were used to having and considered critical to running their respective business units. They had to learn quickly that their new role and function was to operate their terminals, or service centers, based primarily on service criteria, not on balancing their revenue versus expenses. Their performance would be based on the timely pick-up and delivery of the customers freight. Time, not expenses, became their new lifeline to continued employment.

In their new world of FedEx Freight, they would be judged primarily on their on-time service record and how efficiently they managed only their assigned workforce, not their entire operation. I am not saying this is a bad thing, just trying to emphasize that this was an abrupt and major change that no one anticipated during the acquisition process. The terminal managers under Watkins earned quarterly bonus payouts based on their respective unit's performance. Under FedEx Freight, they would earn an annual, one time bonus payout, based on overall company performance, and by the way, the bonus they could earn now with FXNL was smaller than what they could have earned under the Watkins program.

This change also took some time for our entire workforce to adjust to since they were used to knowing how their respective terminals P&L statements, as well as, the entire company as a whole, performed month to month. Under Watkins, all financial information was shared at all levels of the organization. At FedEx Freight, as we were told, being a publicly-held stock company, only company level results were reviewed by the senior management of that company. At the terminal or service center level, managers were actually told not to worry about the profitability of a pick up and delivery run. They should only worry about the number of stops per hour.

"I once heard profit is the applause you get for taking care of customers and your people." - Ken Blanchard - American author and management expert

Differences in titles, responsibilities, status - As mentioned earlier, our senior field leadership, who had been regional vice presidents and officers at Watkins, became managing directors at National. (In a field organization, terminals roll up into geographic districts and districts roll up into geographic regions.) They, along with their respective district managers, were told by the Freight senior leadership that now their primary role with FXNL was to execute the plans delivered to them by senior leadership without much discussion or debate. At Watkins that regional leadership team played a significant role in the development, communication and implementation of the company's operating plan. Now, they were told their role was to comply with directives and execute plans in a supportive and positive manner, regardless of their personal views. Their job, albeit at a higher level, was to meet service standards, just like the terminal managers.

****

"Leaders who make it a practice to draw out the thoughts and ideas of their subordinates and who are receptive even to bad news will be properly informed. Communicate downward to subordinates with at least the same care and attention as you communicate upward to superiors." - L. B. Belker - *business author*

What made the reality of the new world even worse for our field leadership was when they realized that they all had different and lower titles and related perks than their counterparts at Freight East. This meant lower salary grades and pay ranges, smaller bonus plans, smaller stock options and other perks. As explained previously, the managers over an operating region at Freight East and West were vice presidents, with the related officer perks – ours were managing directors, a step down. It was the same scenario for our district managers. At Freight East and West their district managers are managing directors, which is a higher salary grade and bonus plan than a district manager.

We complained almost immediately about the inequity and continued to raise the issue as a serious morale issue over the next 18 months. We were told that the issue could be addressed once we started meeting our financial budget. This justification for such disparities was simply never acceptable to any of us especially since Freight East had effectively taken $100 million in revenue from us without giving us any corresponding long-haul revenue. This, however, was something we had no control over nor did anyone at Freight seem to empathize with our concerns.

****

"One who works for his own profit is likely to work hard. One who works for the use of others, without profit to himself, is likely not to work any harder than he must." - B. Carroll Reece - *American politician from Tennessee*

Differences in expenses, asset allocations, profits - During the first few months following the acquisition, we held an incredible number of meetings across the country with employee groups at all levels. Senior management of both National and Freight spent endless hours answering questions, presenting rebranding plans, providing information on the arrival of the new FedEx uniforms, explaining why there were differences in some of the benefits between the FedEx operating segments and our plans regarding benefits at National and Freight, etc. In addition, there were many visitors from Memphis and Harrison to our General Offices in Lakeland, so they could begin to better understand how we operated and who the various managers were who ran the various departments at National.

At the end of September 2006, the tone of our meetings with FedEx Freight leadership quickly changed from upbeat to somber, as we closed out the FXNL financial statements for the first month. We, Watkins, now FXNL, for the first time in decades, did not meet our financial goals. These were goals that were established by FedEx Freight. Most of the senior management at FedEx Freight were disappointed, but no one more than our senior management team at National. While we believed that the financial group at FedEx Freight anticipated some transition costs, few anticipated that we would miss our budget by the amount we did. The honeymoon was indeed coming to an abrupt end.

As we began reviewing the details for September 2006 and forecasting into the next few months, we realized several things. First, the asset method of our purchase had a direct affect on our cost structure. Before the acquisition, we had many terminal facilities, tractors, trailers, fork lifts and equipment, for example, that were totally depreciated or paid off and had been for years. We had very little debt on our books. This included our 30-acre headquarters complex and downtown office building in Lakeland, as well as a number of very large terminals in prime metropolitan real estate markets all across the country. For example, we had a fully depreciated terminal in a prime California location with a fair market value of $27 million.

When those fully-depreciated, or paid off, assets became FedEx National LTL, they went on the FedEx books at their fair market value. Assets valued at fair market value begin the depreciation process which is an expense that lowers the net income. Add to this the cost of "good will," which is normal in most acquisitions. Besides the fair market value assets, we added all the contractor owned pick-up and delivery equipment that was purchased concurrent with the acquisition as well as, hiring those contractors and their drivers as employees, now with full company benefits. In other words, our stepped up cost basis structure on the new company increased significantly under FedEx, as compared to the cost structure when we were a privately-held company.

Along with having a much higher cost structure, we also now had to pay our share of the FedEx corporate overhead charges. These charges included such things as our share of the FedEx corporate offices, the FedEx Freight Headquarters costs, as well as, paying for things like marketing costs such as the NASCAR racing cars, television ads, sporting events and sports stadium sponsorships, etc. The practice of allocating overhead expenses such as marketing, for example, back to operating units is a very common accounting practice. This was not in any way unique to FedEx. These corporate management fees or charge backs, do benefit each of the operating segments worldwide, but they were significant. Combine the higher cost structure and the magnitude of the management fees, and we realized we faced a very daunting challenge in the months ahead.

****

"The trouble with a budget is that it's hard to fill up one hole without digging another." - Dan Bennett - Ph.D in Mathematics and corporate speaker

Making things worse, as I mentioned previously, it wasn't long after the acquisition that we lost all the regional next-day freight that we had developed at Watkins in the five years before the sale. That $100 million a year freight revenue volume went to Freight East because that type of freight, as we were told, was their business model and they had the processes and systems and sales force to continue supporting it. BUT, we did NOT get any of the long-haul freight revenue and volume that Freight East or West was handling before the acquisition. This obviously affected our profit and loss statement and added to what was already becoming a very complex business challenge - a higher cost structure and little evidence of new revenue from "pent up demand."

****

"Profits, like sausages……are esteemed most by those who know least about what goes into them." - Alvin Toffler - US social commentator and author of Future Shock

Changes in Authority - Following quickly behind the closing of the acquisition, a separate company of the Freight segment, called

Custom Critical, wanted to meet with our line haul operations group to discuss FedEx National LTL transporting some of their shipments through our long haul network which would be a revenue source for us and would help a sister FedEx company in the spirit of collaboration. The vice president of Operations for Custom Critical, along with our director of Marketing and our Line Haul management group met in the Sales Conference Room of our Lakeland offices. That meeting went well and it appeared upon its conclusion that we would be doing beneficial business with another FedEx company. Our line haul group was quickly informed by the line haul department in Harrison that all such negotiations must first go through them. We never did close that deal and a very exciting potential revenue source vanished as quickly as our regional freight did when it was taken by FedEx Freight East. Sadly, a key FedEx principle of operating independently did not extend to its newest separate company of the Freight segment.

Adjusting to Legal - Shortly after Labor Day 2006, we had our first full-time lawyer join our staff in Lakeland as vice president-general counsel. He was an attorney from the Freight offices in Memphis and had also worked for FedEx Express before joining the Freight segment. Having a full time attorney on staff was totally new for us. We, as a privately held company, used outside counsel when we needed legal support or information. Our new general counsel eventually added a staff attorney to his staff, so our legal department in Lakeland went from none to three including the legal secretary.

As we learned quickly, nothing happened until the Legal Department had first reviewed and approved it. Whatever we did regarding customer contracts, written policies, amending policies, practices and procedures, sending out communications of any kind to our work force, employee written performance improvement plans, employee terminations, and all interaction with any government agency, whatever you can imagine in the normal conduct of business, had to first be reviewed by our Legal Department. We were indeed lucky though, since our vice president - general counsel was a very realistic business person who balanced both the legal perspective with the business objectives. We eventually considered him, and his staff, as critical components of our business and vital members of our senior staff organization. We highly valued his perspective and opinion. This was one major change for FXNL that we came to totally appreciate.

Each company within FedEx Freight had its own vice president - general counsel and legal staff, with dotted line reporting relationship to the senior vp general counsel at the FedEx Freight Headquarters in Memphis. The freight segment, as a total, had about twelve attorneys plus support staff. Some offered substantive legal opinions while others seemed focused on changing almost anything up for review to suit their own personal writing style and legal perspectives. Eventually, as previously stated, we accepted our new reality that nothing went on that Legal didn't have final approval over and sign-off authority. **I personally have always believed that attorneys, internal or external, should be business partners, not a final review authority.** As we had learned, our world had changed forever in many ways, this simply being just one aspect.

****

"Well, I don't know as I want a lawyer to tell me what I cannot do. I hire him to tell how to do what I want to do." - J. P. Morgan - *American financier, banker, philanthropist and art collector.*

Many other things continued to change during that first quarter, in spite of being repeatedly told before the closing that nothing was going to change. It is better to tell the workforce that change is inevitable and that they will be kept informed of the needed changes during the transition period. **Never promise a workforce that nothing is going to change.** That simply calls into question your credibility which is then quickly determined to be zero when the inevitable change process begins.

Changes in Employee Recognition and Philanthropy - Recall the Rolex watch award at Watkins for the 20-year service anniversary recognition? That ended when we became FedEx National LTL. We had a number of employees at the time of the acquisition who were in their 20th year of service and were bitterly disappointed to find out they would not be receiving their Rolex watch upon reaching their 20-year anniversary date. The rationale was that the Rolex award was something the Watkins family awarded to long tenured employees. We were no longer Watkins. Regardless of the rationale, our workforce viewed this as an important and significant take away.

As previously mentioned, and while not a significant change, in the scheme of everything else going on, we were no longer able to continue our role as good corporate citizen and to make charitable contributions to non-profit organizations in our hometown of Lakeland, FL. It is important to reference again here considering the financial plan we were now expected to operate under. Our hands seemed to be tied in almost any direction we tried to turn.

The end of October 2006 brought yet another very disappointing financial result for the month. FedEx Freight's senior leadership was beginning to drill down into every line item of our financial report as if to find some revelation as to our shortfall from our budget. Nothing had changed in how we operated from August 2006, the month before we were acquired. But a lot had been changed beyond our control in the first and second month of being owned by FedEx, nonetheless, the concerns were mounting and the scrutiny was intensifying. Where oh where was the revenue from that "pent up demand" that we had heard so much about during the due diligence period and those months leading up to the actual acquisition date? We desperately needed it to cover our higher cost structure.

In November of 2006, the Freight leadership directed us to create a new position - managing director of Financial Planning and Analysis. The only candidate we were given to consider for the position was from Freight East in Harrison. *Now there was a surprise!* We were told that we needed someone on our staff who was familiar with the FedEx accounting and reporting procedures and who could assist us in drilling down into our less than satisfactory financial results. The new managing director - Financial Planning and Analysis, started at FXNL in November 2006 and relocated to Lakeland, FL from Harrison, AR. And to make matters worse, we now had his salary and benefits as additional expenses in addition to his relocation costs to add to our already struggling budget.

Hello! Another wake up call so soon after the acquisition, but this time the undercurrent was that our credibility as efficient operators may now be coming into question. In addition, it was implied that the Freight leadership wanted to have someone in place at FXNL in Lakeland, FL just in case our tenured vice president - Controller left the company. That also implied that Freight leadership had little confidence in the financial staff that we had in place at Watkins for years before the acquisition. If that wasn't their intention, no one in the Freight leadership attempted to assure our FXNL group that they were, indeed, respected financial professionals or trusted by Freight leadership.

****

"Without trust, words become the hollow sound of a wooden gong. With trust, words become life itself." - John Harold - poet

FXNL closed the financial books for November 2006 and again, did not achieve its financial budget goal. This now made three months in a row that we did not perform according to our plan. This would begin to cause serious concerns in any company. FedEx Freight's excitement over acquiring Watkins Motor Lines quickly changed to, what some of us perceived as, resentment. Where oh where was that promised "pent up demand" for our services?

On December 20, 2006, FedEx announced its Earnings Release. The portion on the FedEx Freight Segment stated as follows:

"On September 3, FedEx completed the purchase of Watkins Motor Lines. The operations of Watkins Motor Lines are being rebranded as FedEx National LTL. Operating margin declined during the quarter, as the impact of FedEx National LTL, including integration costs, more than offset the benefit from a property sale gain."

"Less-than-truckload (LTL) shipments increased 28% year over year primarily due to the FedEx National LTL acquisition and demand for FedEx Freight's regional and interregional services. Average daily LTL shipments at FedEx Freight, excluding FedEx National LTL, continued to grow in the second quarter, although growth moderated each month during the quarter. LTL yield improved 11% year over year reflecting higher yields from longer-haul Fedex National LTL shipments and higher rates."

Our Honeymoon was indeed over.

****

"Watch the costs and the profits will take care of themselves."
Andrew Carnegie - Founder of Carnegie Steel (US Steel)

MY CHAPTER 6 - LEADERSHIP "AHA'S"

****

- Do not confuse your customers - they don't care about your problems.
- You CANNOT over plan the details of any organizational change - The Devil is in the Detail!
- A lack of equity at any level of the organization lowers the moral. At multiple levels, it breeds mistrust.
- The closer a person is to directly affecting their bonus earnings the the harder they work to achieve the results that benefit them the most. Tell them they don't have to worry about profits and you diminish their commitment to the organization.
- Corporate attorneys, internal or external, should be business partners, not the final authorities.
- Never promise "… nothing is going to change…" in the organization. In today's challenging world, most people will not believe it anyway and you just look foolish making such a promise.
- Never discourage or stop feedback from, or 2-way communications with, the workforce.
- A repeat - The Cornerstone of an effective Employee Relations Program is Communications.
- Higher costs while reducing revenue does not create profits -DUH!

WHAT ARE YOUR CHAPTER 6 "AHA'S?"

- _____
  _____
- _____
  _____
- _____
  _____
- _____
  _____

WHAT IS YOUR FAVORITE QUOTE?

- _____

_____

And You Call This F-ing Leadership?

Chapter 7

TRANSMOGRIFICATION BEGINS

****

"The worst crime against working people is a company which fails to operate at a profit." - Samuel Gompers - *the first and longest serving president of the American Federation of Labor (AFL).*

Transmogrification is such a unique and descriptive word that I felt it best described what FXNL and its employees went through following the acquisition. This term goes beyond the normal meaning or implication of the often overused term of "change," at least in the traditional sense. Transmogrification is the act of changing into a different form or appearance - it is truly about transformation.

As noted in Chapter 5, and important to mention before going on with this chapter, the president and ceo of FedEx Freight West in San Jose, CA, resigned shortly after our acquisition and went to work for a competitor. This was surprising to us since we had just joined the Freight family of companies, only to see one of its presidents soon depart. As you'll recall, the vacant position was filled by an officer from FedEx Freight East who relocated from Harrison, AR to San Jose, CA. The reality of the American Freightways bias continues to play out later involving this person when our FXNL president retired in 2009.

During late fall of 2006, FedEx Freight in Memphis announced that the Information Technology departments from all three companies (FedEx Freight East, FedEx Freight West, and FedEx National LTL) would be combined under a single leadership structure and would move their reporting structures to Freight System, Inc. effective in January 2007. The System group was organized to mirror the FedEx Services segment. Its goal, like that of FedEx Services, was to consolidate shared services that support the transportation businesses of the Freight segment. Groups like Information Technology, Employee Benefits, and Real Estate, for example, would pool their resources and work together under one common management structure for the common good of all the companies within the Freight segment.

The new Freight System organization created its own, separate Human Resources staff and other necessary support functions to operate as a separate administrative entity of the Freight segment. This meant I had to give up one of my Human Resources managers to join the System organization, as well as my Employee Benefits Department. While I was disappointed to see a good HR manager and my benefits group removed from National's authority, it did make good business sense to manage benefits through one consolidated department.

On January 1, 2007, FXNL's entire Information Technology group, as well as our Employee Benefits and Real Estate departments, started reporting directly to a senior vice president based in Memphis, who was over the System group. The employees remained in their respective locations, but no longer reported to the individual companies.

On January 26, 2007, it was announced that, effective June 1st, of that year, the sales and pricing functions from each Freight operating segment would be consolidated and become a part of FedEx Freight System. This was indeed a good long-term decision that would enhance the customer experience and drive continued growth. Why wait until June was a question asked by many. The customers were becoming increasingly frustrated with the divided sales force, the confusion over the pricing differences, etc.

To make a major acquisition and then not pull some of these functions together until nine months later just didn't seem to make sense to us at the time, especially for the sales organization. We were never told why these consolidation announcements were spaced out nor why the organization had to wait to implement them. Something as major as acquiring a billion dollar trucking company and blending it into the overall operation should have been a top planning priority during the twelve month period leading to the closing of the transaction. What we did assume was that time was needed to train and orient both sales forces and to communicate our developing marketing strategies to our customer base throughout the country.

Also, in January 2007, the managing director of Human Resources at FedEx Freight in the Memphis office, was promoted to vice president of Human Resources reporting directly to the president of FedEx Freight. This, from my perspective, was an excellent move and an indication the human resources function would begin having more influence over the entire Freight segment. The segment very much needed more common policies and procedures on Human Resources, but as long as we had three vice presidents of Human Resources in three different companies, change was not going to happen easily or quickly.

Having a peer functional Human Resources officer at the Freight Headquarters in Memphis meant that the segment would finally have someone to raise the issues and drive the needed change that would eventually result in across-the-segment human resources policies and procedures. We had significant differences among the Freight family of companies in our pay practices and benefit plans and in our procedures on almost everything related to the management of our people. As long as the Memphis based vp of Human Resources had the ear of the Freight president, I was hopeful for some positive changes.

On February 5, 2007, FedEx Freight announced the official launch of its new long-haul less-than-truckload (LTL) service, FedEx National LTL. The release stated "In five-months, we have made tremendous progress in our strategy of providing a reliable and cost-effective service for long-haul shippers." It further stated that FedEx National LTL had also re-engineered its operations to focus on the long-haul market with a strictly scheduled network, similar to FedEx Freight's operations in the regional market. The announcement went on to state that these changes enhanced FedEx National LTL's already strong on-time performance, a key requirement of shippers in all sectors. *Really? A key requirement?* We thought the key request from shippers was for Freight to have a long-haul value proposition to complement its regional business - which is why we were acquired. This key message was an integral part of the dvd message sent to our workforce upon our acquisition by the Freight president.

****

"In preparing for battle I have always found that plans are useless, but planning is indispensable." - Dwight D. Eisenhower, US President and general of the Army.

We had entered calendar year 2007 with increasing trepidation. The months of January, February, and sometimes March, at least in the trucking industry, are normally very slow revenue months. January especially since it follows the Christmas selling season. Retailers are closely trimming their inventories, and manufacturers are managing softer production schedules. Therefore, demand for shipping goods is significantly reduced. To enter a traditionally slow period for the industry and to be struggling with a difficult, if not impossible, budget meant we were not optimistic that things would start getting any better than they had the previous four months. This all came on top of a steady reduction in our ADS (Average Daily Shipment) counts - our customers simply were not responding with the talked about and planned for "pent up demand." Besides all of this, what no one could have foreseen was the beginning of the economic downturn. We started examining every opportunity to reduce our operating costs. Where oh where was that promised pent up demand from our customers?

The biggest challenge in managing slow periods is scheduling dockworker and driver hours. The slower the freight flow becomes, the less work there is for the service center. When we operated as Watkins, we would first ask for volunteers to take a layoff, then if sufficient numbers did not volunteer, we would force the least senior to take layoff. This provided full employment to those remaining and, as soon as normal business volumes resumed, everyone would be back to work on regular working schedules. At FedEx, we were not permitted to "lay off" our employees because that was part of the long established culture. This meant that to keep everyone on the payroll, everyone's workweek had to be reduced. For example, a driver who might have been working 50 hours a week before Christmas might only get 30 hours during January and February. We thought that being restricted from initiating our annual staff reduction program was ridiculous. This in turn effectively punishes the senior employees because everyone's hours get reduced - sort of like spreading the pain around. In reality, the junior employees see their hours cut back to almost nothing, forcing them to apply for unemployment benefits anyway. **Not being able to effectively reduce staff when business levels dictate essentially punishes the entire workforce.**

Allow the entire workforce to pay the price for the sake of public relations or image is a sure way to quickly sink morale. To do so is simply insensitive and doesn't acknowledge the realities of the ebb and flows of today's business cycles. The least senior employees know how business works in down cycles and expect the realities that come with their junior status.

While the ink was still drying from the acquisition, the engineers and line haul/transportation analysts based in the Freight offices in Harrison started making routine visits to our Lakeland offices. They spent countless hours questioning our managers on how our long haul system worked and why we did things the way we did.

We ran our long-haul network, or system, using team drivers who drove sleeper cabs and could drive from origin to destination with minimal stops, regardless of the length of haul. The Freight East and West networks were designed on relay operations using a single driver in a non-sleeper cab. The Freight segment now had two totally different operations - one serving the regional one and two-day freight markets, and one serving the long -haul market. Remember, our being a long-haul carrier is why FedEx presumedly acquired the assets of Watkins Motor Lines - to handle their pent up demand for value oriented long-haul service.

What we couldn't assess at the time was whether they simply didn't understand our model and were trying to learn it, or if they didn't care and wanted to change it to a model that aligned with their mode of operation. The more the visitors came and met with our folks, the more we were convinced that they truly had little interest in listening or learning. Their motives started becoming clear as we entered into January.

In looking back and listening to the DVD that FedEx Freight sent out to employees in early September of 2006 announcing the acquisition, the president of Freight at that time, commented on screen to Chip Watkins: "As you and I have talked....**with just a few adjustments,** I think we can have your network be a dynamite service network to the long-haul industry and work hand-in-hand with FedEx Freight on the regional side and we'll have a value proposition that cannot be met by anyone out there."

The countless lost and nonproductive hours during all those engineering and analysis visits could have been avoided had we simply been told up front that they were going to change our network and that our role now was to support the predetermined network changes and to implement the changes by the desired date.

A special committee was soon formed to "re-engineer" our entire transportation system and line haul network. Just six months following the "nothing is going to change" acquisition of a premier long haul trucking company, the transmogrification process was well underway. We were told that the re-engineering would allow the company to:

- Give consistent 99% on-time reliability to our customers;
- Change to five-day work schedules at all our break bulks and terminals;
- Improve our load average;
- Lower our costs;
- Return the company to its core competency as a nationwide long haul carrier.

The shocking thing to our management team was that no one in the Freight leadership ever asked our team what we might suggest or do to reach any of these goals, yet alone re-engineer the entire nationwide network. As I have stated previously, the arrogance of the Freight senior staff from Harrison did not elicit any two way dialogue - it was simply their way, sweet and simple.

****

"It is greed to do all the talking but not want to listen at all." - Democritus, ancient Greek philosopher.

For many years, Watkins Motor Lines had used a sophisticated software program to model all proposed freight movement transportation system designs before we implemented them. This purchased software program had been tailored to our specific form of operation. It correctly predicted line haul costs and service impacts for each system change as far out as ten years. To us it was an invaluable tool in operating our company efficiently and cost effectively. What shocked us was the fact that the Freight leadership had no interest in our modeling of their desired changes to our transportation system and network. They ignored the model projections of substantial increases in the costs per week in distance and empty miles.

The results of this reliable and quantifiable data was presented to several different Freight officers and their respective staff groups within the Freight leadership team. All to no avail. What was unbelievable to us was that the entire re-engineering effort was mandated to us without any analysis as to the potential effect on our profitability. We were responsible for meeting our FXNL budget, but were totally ignored when we questioned the facts that pointed to increasing our already inflated cost structure. Freight leadership did not consider the projections of increased costs on a re-engineered system that involved increased miles, additional facilities, and new equipment at a time when we were dropping millions in revenue every week.

The FXNL managers were clearly the lone voices in these discussions - Freight leadership clearly wanted FXNL to align the functioning of our long-haul network with the regional network, the facts be damned. This project lasted until it was implemented in July of 2007. In the end, hundreds of our line haul drivers across the country had to relocate to new relay stations or different line haul domiciles, or lose their jobs. One major line haul and maintenance facility was eliminated after we issued the legally required Worker Adjustment and Retraining Notification (WARN) notices. WARN notices are required anytime a permanent workforce reduction occurs involving 50 or more employees. While our drivers were offered very modest relocation allowances, nothing made up for the actual losses many incurred in order to keep their jobs. Many accepted severance payouts and left the company. The title of this book came to my mind many times during this very complex re-engineering project.

****

"There is nothing which rots morale more quickly and more completely than...the feeling that those in authority do not know their own minds."
- Lionel Urwick, Harvard Business Review 1956

In February 2007, Freight leadership raised the issue of FXNL service center managers having company cars. They discovered that the terminal or service center managers at Freight West, as well as our managers, all had company cars. These cars were a part of their jobs when they directly managed their sales representatives and made routine customer visits. The service center managers at Freight East did not have company cars. Since FXNL service center managers no longer had direct responsibility for the sales function, I was instructed to send a memo to our service center managers informing them that they would be losing their company cars. They were told that their cars had to be turned in when their respective leases expired during the time period of March 1, 2007, but not later than May 31, 2008. No specific date was given. Upon turning in their car they would receive an annual salary increase of $7,500. This amount and method of payment was, in my opinion, fair since all future pay increases would be on a higher base salary as well as a higher salary base for bonus calculations. The difficulty was that each manager had to go out and purchase a car and insure it, the first time in years for many of them. There was no way to put lipstick on this pig. It was simply another major change and a significant take-away for all of our service center managers. But, as some told me, they still had a job. Again, the incredible optimism of the human spirit prevailed.

Our average daily shipment count continued to erode, in part, by the confusion created for our customers by our two different sales forces. Our sales force essentially competed for the same customers with pricing differences between our regional and long-haul service products. Compounding the business erosion was a slowing economy. Don't forget the regional freight we had to hand off to Freight East. It goes without saying at this point, FXNL did not meet its budget objectives in either the months of January or February, which in turn meant FXNL did not achieve its budget goal for the Second Fiscal Quarter of the FedEx fiscal year. That meant FedEx National LTL missed both the First Fiscal Quarter goal and the Second Fiscal Quarter goal. A very simple concept to understand - lower revenues coupled with higher costs results in lower or no profits - *DUH!*

****

"The man who complains about the way the ball bounces is likely to be the one who dropped it." - Lou Holtz - *football coach, author and motivational speaker*

In early March of 2007, Chip Watkins resigned from FXNL and returned to the family business. The Watkins family continued to operate three trucking companies and had their eye on starting up a new truck load carrier. Chip's Dad, Buz Watkins, who had been fighting cancer for over a year, was finally given no hope for recovery. During Chip's entire career at Watkins Motor Lines he had never worked directly for his Dad, he had always worked for others. Chip left FXNL and was able to spend quality time with Buz until his death in July of 2007.

On March 21, 2007, FedEx announced its Third Quarter Earnings Release. The portion on the FedEx Freight Segment stated as follows:

"Less-than-truckload (LTL) shipments increased 20% year over year due to the Watkins acquisition (now rebranded as FedEx National LTL). Excluding FedEx National LTL, average daily LTL shipments at FedEx Freight regional were down slightly year over year. LTL yield improved 12% year over year reflecting higher yields from longer-haul FedEx National LTL shipments and higher rates."

"Operating margin declined during the quarter primarily due to operating losses at FedEx National LTL, which resulted from softening volumes and ongoing investments to re-engineer its network. Severe winter weather also impacted operating income and margin."

At FXNL we found this earnings release especially frustrating because we never felt it was necessary to re-engineer our entire company, let alone incur the additional costs to do so. We had had decades of very profitable business with the line haul system that was in place, so, to incur the additional costs, or investments to re-engineer as mandated by FedEx Freight, simply didn't make sound business sense to us. And yes, the trend of softening volumes did have a great deal to do with the slowing of the economy BUT it also had to do with customer confusion and frustration caused by two competing sales groups and to some extent the friction between the city drivers at Freight and FedEx National. In the early months after the acquisition, it was quite common for Freight drivers to attempt, and often succeed at picking up FedEx National freight from a customer's dock that we had in common. This "poaching" of shipments further confused many customers when the FXNL driver would show up for his shipment to pick up. It then angered the customers when they were charged different FXF pricing than the FXNL price they'd been quoted. In some instances Freight drivers heckled National drivers and simply treated our drivers as competitors, instead of fellow team members. It took months for this resentment to subside, but in the meantime it significantly added to the customers' confusion.

Additionally, the actual re-engineering was not scheduled to take place until July so the real costs to re-engineer the network were not yet incurred to their fullest extent. After running a very successful business for decades, it's harder than one can describe to have to see an entire organization sit back and watch this incredible saga unfold before one's eyes. Hence, the title of the book again comes to mind.

Shortly after Chip left the company, Bob Simons was appointed president and ceo of FedEx National LTL. Bob was the executive vice president of Operations at Watkins Motor Lines and retained that responsibility with FXNL upon the acquisition. He had roughly 15 years with the company and had spent most of his non-military career in the trucking industry. Bob was with several major transportation companies before joining Watkins in our West Coast operations. Bob's appointment was very well-received throughout the organization and he had the reputation of being a highly professional and well rounded operator who valued and supported pro-active employee relations programs. He related exceptionally well to the workforce at all levels.

Soon after Bob's appointment, the Freight leadership informed us that we needed to create a new position of vice president of Operations to whom our field organization would report. We were told that we needed someone in place at FXNL who understood the FedEx Freight organization and who could help us assimilate more quickly into the operational standards of Freight, as well as help us to integrate the technology that we would be operating under in the future. The candidate was a vice president of Division Operations at FedEx Freight East. *Now there was a surprise!* The really sad reality for us was that we had five region managing directors who had been operations officers with Watkins Motor Lines before the acquisition, but to our knowledge, none of them was considered by Freight leadership for the new position.

Our new vice president of Operations relocated to our Lakeland, FL headquarters and started working in June 2007. Our officer staff now had to accept the reality that Bob Simons' boss, the Freight EVP & COO based in Harrison, would have a FXNL officer loyal primarily to him. The one thing we never had to spend much time on at Watkins was corporate politics. That had all changed now and our new reality as we saw it was always having to look over our shoulders to avoid the ugly reality of Freight segment politics.

The message to us by Freight leadership placing an outside officer at FXNL was that they lacked confidence in us to run our operation independently. This placement resulted in a steady loss of trust by us in our Freight leadership. The lack of trust was new to how we had operated for years as Watkins. This changed all the dynamics of effective two way communications and the critical give and take necessary in any progressive working relationship. How sad, that just eight months following the acquisition, our optimism and trust were quickly fading. While the new officer now embedded into our operation was a hardworking and devoted transportation professional with a long career in the trucking industry, he was, from the standpoint of our company culture, an outsider. To make things worse, an outsider who came from FedEx Freight East. The additional bitter coating on this already distasteful pill was that we also had to absorb the additional expenses of his salary, benefits, and relocation costs.

****

"The moment there is suspicion about a person's motives, everything he does becomes tainted." - Mahatma Gandhi - Indian Philosopher and political leader

In June of 2007, Clay Watkins decided to leave FXNL and return to the Watkins Trucking Group. No member of the Watkins family was working at FXNL which left a strange feeling in the air for many of our long service employees. The times were certainly changing and changing quickly. The workforce was becoming numb to everything happening so fast and they were quickly coming to the reality that literally everything was going to change. For many, for the first time in years, it wasn't fun coming to work anymore. Anxiety and fear of the unknown were slowly creeping in to almost everything we were trying to accomplish. Our world had transformed forever.

What frustrates me even today as I write this, is realizing that most employees in a corporate workforce expect major changes with any acquisition. This reality is simply a given in the world today. However, in this case, the Watkins workforce had been programmed for decades to totally believe the word of senior management - especially when the culture was promoted and reinforced by Watkins family members and their team of leaders. For FedEx Freight to promise such a workforce that nothing was going to change was, to me, simply irresponsible. FedEx Freight had almost a full year to study and understand the Watkins company culture during the due diligence period before the acquisition. They clearly did not understand our culture, or they didn't care. My strong opinion is that a highly reputable company owes its new workforce as much truth and reality up front while asking the new employees for patience and time as the transition period evolves. **Clear, concise, truthful and straightforward communications is critical in building trust in a workforce.** To do otherwise is simply deceitful.

****

"To have his path made clear for him is the aspiration of every human being in our beclouded and tempestuous existence." - Joseph Conrad, Polish author and novelist in psychological realism.

During the spring of 2007, the FXNL Employee Communications Department was consolidated with the other Freight company communications departments and assigned to the

Freight System organization. Then, in June of 2007, the FXNL Pricing Department and entire sales organization was combined with those respective departments of Freight East and Freight West and assigned to the Freight System organization under a consolidated management structure. This meant that FXNL no longer had responsibility for the IT, Real Estate, Benefits, Employee Communications, Sales and the Pricing functions. FXNL, as a separate company within the Freight segment, was now primarily just an operations function. While this was an abrupt change to what we were told and envisioned during the acquisition process, to me it was a good sign that there was going to be more centralized focus on some of the key support functions that would benefit the entire Freight segment.

As previously discussed, no one at FXNL believed that FedEx Freight needed to incur the ongoing expenses to integrate its network. But, as we had grown accustomed to saying routinely, **"It is what it is."** The line haul re-engineering effort was concluded and implemented systemwide in July 2007. Many drivers either relocated or left their families and had to rent trailers or sleep in campers during the work week so they could keep their jobs. Others simply took their severance and left. Our entire organization developed a survivalist mentality - do whatever is necessary to keep a job until the dust settles. Many believed that time would sort everything out eventually. I so love and admire the human spirit.

The need to adopt a survival mentality truly hit home for everyone when our vice president of Transportation was terminated during the re-engineering project. During the project planning phase, he passionately expressed his concerns about the viability of the new network, with the placement of many of the relay stations, with some of the assumptions on the projected savings, and with the findings of our software program indicating higher costs, etc. Freight leadership resented his uncooperativeness and dissent. Eventually they suggested to his boss, Jeff Baker, senior vice president of Operations for FXNL, and Bob Simons, the new president of FXNL, that he be replaced. With Bob being new in his position, and Jeff wanting a fully supportive and engaged staff officer moving forward, they both agreed to replace our Transportation vp. They believed, which I support in theory, that **any officer has the right to have people on their staff who best support that officer's goals and those of the**

organization. This particular officer simply wanted to be heard and wanted the opportunity to present objective facts that were supported by quantitative measurement criteria.

****

"My only objective is to isolate your stupidity." - David A.J. Axson, author of *The Management Mythbuster*

In addition to supporting the belief of an officer's right to their own staff, **I also believe that anyone at any level of an organization has the right to fair and objective due process.** I did not support this termination and became vocal about my concerns to Jeff, Bob and his boss at Freight. I was told that the final decision was ultimately ours to make. Not believing for a second that Bob or Jeff had any options, I called the vp of Human Resources at Freight in Memphis to register my concerns. Shocking to me was that HR in Memphis did not know anything about this potential termination of an officer of the company. After the group in Memphis worked through some issues with the group in Harrison, eventually our vp was terminated. As a result of how this was initially handled, the procedures changed where Freight-Memphis Human Resources and Freight-Memphis Legal had to be involved with all officer and managing director performance issues going forward. In the end, we lost a good, long-term employee simply because he was not supportive of the Freight direction or directives regarding our re-engineering.

To me, if a company has plans to make changes to its organization, make those plans clear up front, don't go through the facade of eliciting feedback when in reality, none is wanted. **I much prefer a benevolent dictator to a deceitful manipulator.** I have worked for both and much prefer the benevolent and caring dictator. You clearly know where they stand and what they expect from you. Generally, they are trustworthy and that, above all else, is critical to a healthy and productive work environment.

If anything good could have come from losing a long term employee, it was that a highly respected field operations managing director from FXNL and previously an officer with Watkins, was promoted to fill the vacancy. We were not required to bring in an officer from FedEx Freight East. Our new vice president of

Transportation brought new insight and perspective to the position and worked tirelessly to make the new system work as best it could. Admittedly, it is much easier to assume someone else's command and initiate the change process than to change the one you have built and are emotionally tied to.

I share this in more detail than is probably necessary because the event did send a significant message across the bow of our entire organization. The message was loud and clear - candid, two-way communication between our group and the Freight leadership was not encouraged, or appreciated, or supported, even at the officer level. Our belief in the value of two way communications had been chiseled away.

****

"Exemplary leaders reward dissent. They encourage it. They understand that whatever momentary discomfort they experience as a result of being told they might be wrong, it is more than offset by the fact that the information will help them make better decisions." - Warren Bennis - American scholar and organizational consultant.

Perhaps even more sad, made so by their shear numbers, was that our employees felt this way too. As a leader, don't make the mistake of equating working at or for an hourly wage with a lack of either intellectual or emotional intelligence. Our employees were reading between the lines of the positive faces all our mangers were trying to put on these events as they were taking place. Despite our best explanations they saw how the winds were blowing, many of them even before we did.

As we moved through the summer of 2007, I sensed a lasting change in the overall spirit and morale among the officer and managing director staff. While any group of people working together can experience periods of low energy or low enthusiasm, this was very different. Most of us were coming to grips with the reality that the Freight leadership truly didn't want to listen to our ideas or evaluate our suggestions or take into account our thoughts on almost anything we had to offer. We were not a group who easily sat back and waited to be told what to do. We were a group who helped build the Watkins organization into a billion dollar nationwide trucking company that was highly respected in the marketplace.

All of our mid and senior level managers, over time, started feeling like broken dogs chained in the back yard and who had to act happy when the master came out at feeding time. We were quickly learning that if we were going to survive with the FedEx Freight segment, we all needed to fall in line and do what we were told to do.

On June 20, 2007, FedEx announced its Fourth Quarter Earnings Release. The portion on the FedEx Freight Segment stated as follows:

"Less-than-truckload (LTL) shipments increased 16% year over year due to the acquisition of Watkins (now rebranded as FedEx National LTL). Excluding FedEx National LTL, average daily LTL shipments at FedEx Freight regional were down slightly year over year, as the slower economy continued to negatively impact demand. LTL yield improved 11% year over year, reflecting higher yields from longer-haul FedEx National LTL shipments, higher rates and favorable contract renewals. A general rate increase was implemented April 2, 2007."

"Operating margins declined primarily due to operating losses at FedEx National LTL, which resulted from softening volumes and ongoing expenses to integrate its network."

And so it continued with softening volumes, a higher operating cost structure, ongoing expenses to integrate our network, and a workforce that was becoming numb over the torturous barrage of constant changes, coupled with the reality that operating independently was not achievable. All only made worse by the inability to be a profitable company within the FedEx Freight segment. There is neither joy nor pride in being in last place or in being perceived as a disappointment or, worse, a failure.

****

"In business, the earning of a profit is something more than an incident of success. It is an essential condition of success. It is an essential condition of success because the continued absence of profit itself spells failure."
- Louis Dembitz Brandeis - lawyer and Supreme Court Justice.

MY CHAPTER 7 - LEADERSHIP "AHA'S"

****

- Not everything that is good for public relations or the media is good for employee relations.
- Always remember the importance that organizational culture plays in the long term success of any organization.
- Profits can only happen when all employees work together.
- A fully informed and engaged workforce is essential for long term business success.
- Managers deserve to have knowledgeable employees who fully support the manager's and organization's objectives and goals.
- Benevolent dictators make better bosses than deceitful manipulators.
- A prolonged and drawn out change process saps the energy, enthusiasm and commitment from the workforce.
- Building trust with the workforce and the customers is essential in leadership. Without trust, no organization can survive long term.
- Trust is the foundation and a fundamental ingredient in sound organizational health.

WHAT ARE YOUR CHAPTER 7 "AHA'S?"

- _____
- _____
- _____
- _____

WHAT IS YOUR FAVORITE QUOTE?

- _____

And You Call This F-ing Leadership?

Chapter 8

TRANSMOGRIFICATION CONTINUES

****

"In any culture, subculture, or family in which belief is valued above thought, and self-surrender is valued above self-expression, and conformity is valued above integrity, those who preserve their self-esteem are likely to be heroic exceptions."
- Nathaniel Branden - author and psychotherapist

No quote could better describe the many employees at FXNL at this stage in the transmogrification of FXNL. Being able to preserve their self-esteem, given the highest level of negative change in our 75 year old culture, was simply heroic. The transmogrification was continuing at a rapid pace with no end in sight. Recall, transmogrification is the process of complete and usually extreme or grotesque change from one state or form to another. This chapter highlights the continuing process of endless change, disappointments and broken promises.

August of 2007 was mostly spent adjusting to the new reality that we had just dismantled the entire line haul and transportation system that had successfully been used for decades at Watkins Motor Lines. Don't forget, the Watkins line haul system was designed to provide nation-wide long-haul transportation services and was the very reason that FedEx purchased the company. It was to provide a "value proposition" to FedEx Freight customers and would be servicing the "pent-up demand" for such services. Never before had our entire workforce been through such a gut-wrenching change process, and we all were looking forward to some time to catch our breath and recharge our attitudes for the challenges we faced due to our higher operating costs and declining revenues. That was indeed a very short-lived fantasy.

On September 17, 2007, we announced a field reorganization going from five operating regions to three. As the communications stated, the merger of the FedEx Freight and FedEx National sales groups under the FedEx Freight System umbrella on June 1, as well as the efficiencies gained from the re-engineering on July 23 lead to this restructuring. As our workforce was told, this was done to maximize our efficiencies so that we could ensure 99% on-time service to our customers. This reduction in the number of regions and districts obviously directly affected those respective regional staff, but also represented another major change that affected reporting relationships, further shaking the ground un the field employees feet. The terminals were now grouped to match the freight flow process.

On September 20, 2007, FedEx announced its First Quarter Earnings Release. The portion on the FedEx Freight Segment stated as follows:

"Less-than truckload (LTL) shipments increased 13% year over year due to the acquisition of Watkins (now rebranded as FedEx National LTL), partially offset by lower average daily shipments at FedEx Freight regional. FedEx Freight regional shipments declined slightly, as demand has been restrained by the slower U.S. economy. Effective July 23, 2007, FedEx Freight reduced its standard regional LTL fuel surcharge by 25% and FedEx National LTL revised its standard LTL fuel surcharge to levels commensurate with FedEx Freight. Despite the fuel surcharge reduction, LTL yield improved 8% year over year, reflecting higher yields from longer-haul FedEx National LTL shipments."

"Operating margins declined during the quarter due to operating losses at FedEx National LTL and lower year over year growth in regional yield, including the impact from the fuel surcharge reduction. While the LTL fuel surcharge reduction is expected to have a negative impact on revenue and earnings

for the remainder of the fiscal year, this change is expected to strengthen FedEx Freight competitively and drive incremental volumes over the long-term."

So what does all this mean in real numbers? The overall Freight segment revenue of $1.23 billion was up 22% from the prior year's $1.01 billion thanks to FXNL now being in the mix. Operating income of $105 million was down 30% from $150 million the prior year. The operating margin of 8.5% was down from 14.8% the previous year. As for FXNL, our operating costs were up, our revenue was down and quickly eroding by the month. This was further exasperated when we were required to lower the fuel surcharge to our customers. To most of us on the FXNL senior staff, this was quickly turning into a train wreck, and we felt like we were chained to our seats in the passenger coach car with very little chance for survival.

We still had not achieved our monthly or quarterly financial goals at FXNL since the day of our acquisition. What made our declining revenue situation even worse was the fact that the combining of the sales forces didn't seem to be cultivating the "pent-up demand" for long-haul services. In fact, we discovered that most of the regional sales reps were not selling FXNL freight nor did they have goals for selling our services. Our former FXNL sales reps, who were now working under the new System consolidated sales organization, struggled to build up our long-haul revenue and the pricing differences were still a work in progress.

During the fall of 2007, one of the senior officers of the FedEx Freight segment made a visit to our offices in Lakeland. During these regular visits, they would meet one-on-one with various officers to discuss a variety of topics and to establish a more comfortable working relationship. I was included on the schedule for this particular visit, so I prepared a two-page list of my issues and concerns and gave him a copy when we met. He asked me how things were going so far. I told him that we had reduced the bonus levels of our managers, taken away their P&L responsibility, taken away their cars, removed their salesforce from their direct control and reduced their involvement with long term customers, and that we were experiencing manager turnover at levels never seen before. We chatted about the list and went back and forth on a variety of topics.

While we were wrapping up our meeting he made the most preposterous statement I could have ever imagined. He told me that there was a growing concern that the Watkins books may not have revealed a totally accurate reflection of operating costs, especially since we had not achieved our financial objectives since the acquisition over a year ago. I was totally surprised by this statement and its implications. I couldn't believe a senior level officer would express this, even if there were some questions at the highest levels. This statement to me also called into question the due diligence work of FedEx Corporation's own merger and acquisition staff, the many internal and external lawyers who were involved, the FedEx Freight due diligence team, and the Watkins outside legal firm, yet alone the many successful audits conducted through the years by outside major accounting firms. It was unimaginable to imply that this large group of professionals could have done less than a professional job of reporting the status of Watkins financial information and records. At this point, I lost total respect for and trust in this person. **The military taught me that we have to respect the rank of an individual, but that doesn't automatically apply to the person holding the rank. They have to earn the level of respect and trust that goes with the rank they hold.**

As the next few months unfolded, comments were shared by other officers and senior management that indicated that I was not the only one who had heard from Freight leadership on this topic. This type of thinking and its implications was so preposterous that it made me wonder how far the FXF senior leadership would go to put a positive spin on our situation so as to make FXF look good. It certainly solidified my growing doubt as to their integrity.

Shortly after this one-on-one meeting, I got a phone call from my counterpart at FedEx Freight in Harrison. I had known her before she was recruited by FedEx Freight East to be their vice president of Human Resources. She wanted to give me a heads up that I was beginning to get the reputation among the Freight staff in Harrison as a negative person and was not being perceived as a team player. Since she had known me in our roles before FedEx and since we had a high degree of respect for each other, she thought it was important that I know so I could soften my communications style and approach. This call obviously disappointed me with the reality that my long established management style was becoming a liability. My method of providing objective feedback and my candid opinion on running our business had to change. My boss, Bob Simons, also suggested that in our new world, the Freight leadership didn't care what we at FXNL thought, so why expose myself to the risks associated with candid feedback. Obviously one FXNL officer had already proven that candid feedback came with a high price.

****

"Leadership is solving problems. The day soldiers stop bringing you their problems is the day you have stopped leading them. They have either lost confidence that you can help or concluded you do not care. Either case is a failure of leadership." - Colin Powell - Secretary of State and chairman of the Joint Chiefs of Staff.

In less than two weeks after we announced the re-organization of the operating regions, we announced a major staffing adjustment to the FXNL organization through which we would eliminate a number of hourly and salaried positions as a result of the recent system re-engineering. We explained that the re-engineering affected the flow of freight in our system by leveling the volume over the new Monday through Friday service cycle. It also altered the amount of freight being handled - some locations were now processing more, while others were handling less. The volume of freight was also declining rapidly as the economy continued to weaken.

Staffing levels are determined by the number of man hours required to move a certain volume of freight over certain time periods. The re-engineering, decreased the number of man hours needed over seven days to five days to process that set volume of freight. Therefore, some hourly and supervisory positions in almost every FXNL location across the country were eliminated. Since drivers can work freight across docks in addition to driving, they were now used to backfill many of the dockworker positions that were eliminated. Relying on driver job flexibility is a very logical business decision and one that was fully utilized at Freight East. The difficulty at FXNL was making our drivers shift from a traditionally driver only role to one that involved dock work and other duties. It took time to convince our drivers that this was the future and one they needed to embrace if they wanted to continue with FXNL.

On November 18, 2007, the local newspaper, The Lakeland Ledger, ran an article to update readers on the status of the Watkins

Motor Lines acquisition. The headlines read: "FedEx Move Into Lakeland Smooth, Officials Say." *Really?* Has anything I have written so far in this book indicated a smooth transition? Bob Simons, our new president at the time, and his boss, the evp and coo of FedEx Freight, were interviewed. They discussed the rebranding process on all our buildings and equipment, why Chip and Clay had left, Bob's appointment, and they stated that there had been no layoffs in Lakeland. In Lakeland! No reference was made about our field organization where we had either disrupted hundreds of lives or terminated employees unable to relocate as a result of our re-engineering efforts. I have always admired the marketing genius of the FedEx Corporation and their ability to orchestrate a very positive image in the market place. Just an amazing article considering many of the Lakeland based employees knew the number of people and jobs that had been lost in the field. The article had a very positive spin while many of the local charities in Lakeland were asking me why Fedex National LTL could no longer support the local community. The spin was more important than the actual facts despite the fact that many of the Lakeland employees would tell their family, friends and neighbors the truth of the matter. Such a blatant spin in the face of reality of living in a small southern town further eroded the employees' trust and respect in FedEx Freight.

On December 20, 2007, FedEx announced its Second Quarter Earnings Release. The portion on the FedEx Freight Segment stated as follows:

"Less-than-truckload shipments declined 6% year over year, as demand for services in the LTL sector has been restrained by the weak U.S. economy. LTL yield improved 4% year over year, as higher rates and higher yields from longer-haul shipments more than offset the impact of FedEx Freight reducing its fuel surcharge on July 23, 2007."

"Operating income and margin declined during the quarter due to the decline in LTL shipments. The net impact of higher fuel costs and the fuel surcharge reduction also negatively affected margins. Last year's second quarter results included a gain related to the sale of an operating facility and insurance proceeds associated with Hurricane Katrina. While the reduction in the LTL fuel surcharge is expected to have a negative impact on revenue for the remainder of the fiscal year, this change is expected to strengthen FedEx Freight competitively and drive incremental shipments over the long term."

This was the first earning release in which FedEx National LTL was not mentioned at all. We had finally been folded into the Freight segment as a part of the overall report. While we continued to miss our financial objectives for each month and the quarter, it was refreshing to not see us referenced in any way. And as we now know from a historical perspective, the great recession officially began in December 2007. A little known fact outside of the transportation industry is that the trucking industry is the canary in the mine - warning of poisonous fumes of a declining economy six to twelve months before the economy hits bottom.

In January 2008, one of our field district managers in the Southern Region announced his retirement. He had spent decades with Watkins Motor Lines as a terminal, district manager and vice president region manager. He was in many ways an icon to our culture of respecting employee involvement and nurturing team work at all levels. At his retirement party on the dock of the Lakeland Service Center he stated that he would very much miss all the employees he had worked so closely with through the years, but he would not miss FedEx Freight. Most standing there chuckled. It saddened me to realize that this group of employees who once so looked forward to joining the FedEx family of companies now totally related to the sentiments of this long-tenured leader.

We once again reorganized the regions and the alignment of districts within the regions, which resulted in an opening for a managing director of regional operations. And to no one's surprise, our new vice president of Operations, the one who came to us from FedEx Freight East, wanted one of his managing directors from Freight East to fill the position. This move was obviously strongly endorsed by Freight leadership. So, after a series of what I refer to as "cosmetic interviews," a managing director of regional operations from FedEx East was transferred to FXNL as the new managing director of Southern Regional Operations. Not one of the existing district managers from FXNL was considered for the position and all of our field employees knew it. The Freight leadership very much wanted their people to become embedded in the FXNL operation, competence and experience of anyone at FXNL be damned.

On March 1, 2008, the sr. vp and cfo of Freight in Memphis was promoted to executive vice president of Finance and Administration

& cfo and continued his responsibilities over the finance and accounting functions and a large portion of the Freight System organization. He also assumed responsibility over the Human Resources function which meant the FedEx Freight vice president of Human Resources would no longer report directly to the president of the Freight segment. This was not a good thing from my perspective.

Throughout my 43-year career in Human Resources management, I have strongly believed that the Human Resources function must report directly to the head person of any unit - be it a plant operation, a division or a corporation. If the Human Resources function is to have a credible seat at the table, so to speak, then the function needs to have an equal power and authority base as the other functions do. If Finance, Accounting, Legal, Sales and Marketing report to the president, then Human Resources should as well IF the function is perceived as essential and valuable and IF the company proclaims that the employees truly are important and the key to the success of the organization. Having Human Resources report up through the Finance function to the segment president dilutes the direct impact that the function should have on a host of key strategy issues. If at FedEx Freight, "People First" is a credible mantra, then the function, in my opinion, should report directly to the segment president as it does at the Express segment, the Ground segment, the Office segment and the Corporation. **Actions do speak louder than words.**

On March 20, 2008, FedEx announced its Third Quarter Earnings Release. The portion on the FedEx Freight Segment stated as follows:

"LTL shipments declined 3% year over year, as demand for these services continues to be restrained by the weak U.S. economy, although average daily LTL shipments improved sequentially throughout the quarter. LTL yield improved 5% year over year as higher rates, including the impact of the January rate increase, more than offset the July 2007 fuel surcharge reduction."

"Operating income and margin decreased in the quarter due to the net impact of higher fuel costs and the fuel surcharge reduction, higher utilization of purchased transportation and fewer long-haul shipments."

Obviously, the reference to fewer long-haul shipments was a direct reference to FXNL and our rapidly declining average daily shipments. The failing economy and the lingering confusion in the marketplace over the differences between regional and long-haul business and all that went with that resulted in less revenue and yet another FXNL financial failure. Of course, the Freight sales representatives' resistance to selling FXNL long-haul services only added to this worsening revenue situation.

In May 2008, we announced a change of operations throughout FXNL, eliminating four service centers and the reassigning of their respective employees, if they desired to relocate. Changes in our dispatch system and procedures, coupled with a continual decline in average daily shipments, also meant we needed to realign many of our line haul runs and reposition drivers throughout the network. Closing four service centers sent a huge shock wave through our system. While line haul run changes are not unusual in the trucking business, coupled with everything else that had occurred in the previous 12 months, this formal change of operations meant more negative change and uncertainty for the entire workforce. Unmanageable? No. More stress and uncertainty for our entire workforce? Absolutely.

What was troubling to us at FXNL was that we had recommended closing more service centers than the four that were approved. We did an analysis of the average daily shipments at the smaller service centers and had determined that it cost us more to keep some of them operational than we were making in profit. But, within the Freight segment bureaucracy, we had to have all decisions like this reviewed and signed off on by the Marketing Department. They only agreed on and approved the four we closed. They did not want us to take "dots off the map" from a marketing standpoint. Here we were, not one month had we attained our financial goals, the recession was digging deeper and deeper into our average daily shipment count, and we had to dance with the Marketing Department. We never understood why someone in Freight leadership wouldn't bring some sound business logic to the outcome of this review process.

****

"Don't blame the marketing department. The buck stops with the chief executive." - John D. Rockefeller - founder of the Standard Oil Company

On June 18, 2008, FedEx announced its Fourth Quarter Earnings Release. The portion on average daily shipments and financials was unremarkable. What was remarkable was stated as follows:

"On January 1, 2009, FedEx Freight will close its San Jose, Calif. general office. The general office for the combined regional LTL operations will be located in Harrison, Ark. This move will drive efficiencies and enhance the customer experience. The cost of this move will be immaterial to financial results. FedEx National LTL will continue to serve the long haul market as a separate operating company with its general office in Lakeland, Fla."

WOW! Now that announcement sent a tremendous shock wave through the entire Freight segment workforce. To many, this was more shocking because the leadership at Freight in Memphis had vowed over many years that they would never close the San Jose general office. While it was a good sound business decision that was prompted by the lease expiring on the San Jose offices, nonetheless, it was received by many in the workforce as a huge broken promise. How many times do I have to say this: **Never promise a workforce that nothing is going to change. NEVER!**

The new reality for FXNL was that FedEx Freight West, the first trucking company to be acquired in the Freight segment, was being merged into the operation and management of FedEx Freight East. Regardless of what was stated in the earnings release, the seeds of legitimate paranoia were now firmly planted throughout FedEx National LTL. The employees of FXNL had been bitterly taught by the FedEx Freight leadership that their promises were not credible. "How long does FXNL have…" was a growing question among our workforce, despite our repeated attempts to assure them that we would remain a separate operating company.

On September 18, 2008, FedEx announced its First Quarter Earnings Release. The portion on the FedEx Freight Segment stated as follows:

"Less-than-truckload (LTL) average daily shipments increased 4% year over year due to market share gains despite the weak U.S. economy and a competitive pricing environment. LTL yield improved 5% year over year primarily due to increased fuel surcharges."

"Operating results decreased in the quarter due to the weak economy and the competitive pricing environment. There was one fewer operating day in this year's first quarter."

In short, Freight segment revenue was up 10% from last year, operating income was down 15%, and operating margin was down 8.5% from the previous year. The worst of the recession was finally taking its toll on every business across the country, and we faced some significant challenges, as did the entire trucking industry. The pricing environment was vicious and brutal. We, like many trucking companies, were facing a fight for survival.

With a terrible economy and our already poor financial performance as the backdrop, in October 2008, we announced the elimination of all our full-time dock workers at most of our service centers. Only our larger hubs and three major metro service center operations were exempt. The cross dock operation had changed significantly since the acquisition, meaning either our city drivers or a core part-time dockworker group could handle the daily freight moving in and out of the service centers. We announced that our full-time dock workers could transfer to a hub location at their own expense, commit to participation in the driver development program if they were interested in becoming a truck driver, or accept a severance payout.

This was gut wrenching for many of our long-term dock workers, some of whom had over 15 or 20 years of service with the company. Some transferred to hubs (large freight consolidation centers), some entered the driver development program, but many more accepted a severance package and left the company. This was no doubt one of the most emotional and significant changes within our operation since the acquisition, because it literally touched the soul of almost every end-of-line service center. To see dockworkers walking out who had received Rolex watches for their long service to Watkins was heart-breaking. Some simply couldn't become drivers for a host of legitimate reasons, or uproot their families and relocate to a hub. So out the door they went as our transmogrification continued.

****

"Always recognize that human individuals are ends, and do not use them as means to your end." - Immanuel Kant - a German philosopher and author

Just when I didn't think our cost cutting could reach new lows, it did. The decision was made to issue the "2008 Wrap-up" issue of the Dispatcher magazine in black and white and to hand deliver it to employees to take home rather than mailing it to their homes. This company magazine had been produced in color since the late 1980's and mailed to employees' homes since the early 1990's. This change would keep our per copy cost to 34 cents, as opposed to $1.25. I compared this to a family struggling to pay the electric bill by digging through the couch for loose pocket change.

Near the end of December 2008, we presented Freight leadership with a summary of adjustments that we had made to facilities, equipment, technology, and people during the 28 months since our acquisition. These adjustments were made to adjust for the volume reductions, network re-engineering and changes to the management structure. Average daily shipments dropped 29.7%. We reduced full-time dock employees by 40.3%; reduced full-time city drivers by 32.3%; reduced full-time clerical by 40.8%; reduced full-time salaried by 25.3% not counting the 626 salaried employees that were transferred to Freight System; and reduced line-haul drivers by 3.5%. We reduced our total full-time and part-time workforce during those 28 months by 27.8% not counting the total of 971 that transferred to Freight System. We eliminated 1800 driver contractors and their drivers.

These staffing adjustments had been implemented in multiple phases, including the following events:
- 9/06 - Acquisition eliminated 1,000 city driver contractors;
- 7/07 - Re-engineering eliminated two hubs and realigned the line haul driver network;
- 9/07 - Eliminated two operating regions and two districts;
- 10/07 - Second phase of re-engineering to reduce salaried and hourly positions throughout the field organization;
- 5/08 - Eliminated four service centers;
- 7/08 - Combined four service centers;
- 11/08 - Eliminated four service centers and combined the field city and line haul dispatch functions.

During the 28-month process, in spite of the initial increased operating costs from the management fees and stepped up asset valuations, FXNL had saved several millions of dollars in costs. Our field organization had increased efficiencies and improved their on-time delivery service from already good numbers in the 94-95% range up to 97-98%. Some of the FXF operations leadership actually told our field personnel they had done everything asked of them and had done it faster and better than expected. During the process, however, FXNL had totally transformed from the long-haul carrier that FedEx purchased to a company that had no resemblance to its original form, but one that FedEx Freight wanted. The transmogrification process had resulted in a complete and extreme change, one that was considered, by some, as simply grotesque. Obviously, the promised, planned and much needed "pent up demand" never happened and the economy was tanking quickly. The prospects of FXNL reaching their financial objectives was almost impossible at this point. The mood was indeed somber.

On December 18, 2008, FedEx announced its Second Quarter Earnings Release. This release announced broad cost cutting actions across all operating segments due to the weak economy.

"Our financial performance is increasingly being challenged by some of the worst economic conditions in the company's 35-year operating history. We are managing our costs and taking full advantage of market opportunities, and our team members are delivering every day on our promise to make every customer experience outstanding. However, with the decline in shipping trends during our second quarter and the expectation that economic conditions will remain very difficult through calendar 2009, we are taking additional actions necessary to help offset weak demand, protect our business and minimize the loss of jobs."

<u>Cost Reductions</u>
FedEx has already taken actions to reduce over $1 billion of expenses for all of fiscal 2009, including:
- *Elimination of variable compensation payouts*
- *Hiring freeze*
- *Volume-related reductions in labor hours and line-haul expenses*
- *Discretionary spending cuts*
- *Personnel reductions at FedEx Freight and FedEx Office*

FedEx is now implementing a number of additional cost reduction initiatives to mitigate the effects of deteriorating business conditions, including:

- *Base salary decreases, effective January 1, 2009*
  -20% reduction for FedEx Corp. CEO Frederick W. Smith
  -7.5%-10.0% reduction for other senior FedEx executives
  -5.0% reduction for remaining U.S. salaried exempt personnel
- *Elimination of calendar 2009 merit-based salary increases for U.S. salaried exempt personnel*
- *Suspension of 401(k) company matching contributions for a minimum of one year, effective February 1, 2009*

These additional actions are expected to reduce expenses by $200 million during the remainder of fiscal 2009 and approximately $600 million in fiscal 2010. In addition to these actions, each operating company is evaluating other measures should business conditions further deteriorate."

The section of the earning release dealing with just the FedEx Freight segment stated:

"Less-than-truckload (LTL) average daily shipments decreased 2% year over year, as market share gains were more than offset by the weakening U.S. economy. LTL yield declined 1%, as higher fuel surcharges were offset by the effects of a competitive pricing environment."

"Operating income and margin decreased in the quarter due to the competitive pricing environment and lower average daily shipments, partially offset by the benefits from lower variable incentive compensation and continued cost containment initiatives, including the alignment of staffing to current volume levels."

Yes, the times were getting very ugly. For the quarter, FXNL clearly did not meet its financial objectives - *duh!* The entire FedEx Freight segment revenue was down 3% year over year while operating income was down 59% and operating margin was down 6.4%. The world around us was deteriorating at a rapid pace, and fears of job security seemed to dominate almost every conversation. We were truly entering the most challenging business environment since the Great Depression of the 1930's. For those of us at FXNL, a company that had not achieved any of its financial objectives since the acquisition in 2006, we came to work every day completely fearing the unknown and the uncertainty that the new economic and corporate environment represented. The fight for survival dominated the thinking of everyone and, for the first time, we at FXNL felt that the entire FedEx enterprise was in this fight together.

****

"What we need to do is learn to work in the system, by which I mean that everybody, every team, every platform, every division, every component is there not for individual competitive profit or recognition, but for contribution to the system as a whole on a win-win basis." - W. Edwards Deming - statistician, professor, author, lecturer and father of the quality revolution

MY CHAPTER 8 - LEADERSHIP "AHA'S"

****

- Don't wait for a period of calm - leaders must constantly push for continuous improvement.
- Don't torture the workforce with constant changes. Group major changes into specific time blocks that are spaced out into major business cycles or periods.
- Never blame your predecessors for current business problems or failures. You and you alone are responsible for what is happening now.
- You must **EARN** the respect and trust that goes with your position and title.
- The Human Resources function should always report to the top position in the organization.
- Never let the marketing department make the final decisions in running your business.
- Never promise employees that nothing will change. **NEVER!**

WHAT ARE YOUR CHAPTER 8 "AHA'S?"

- _____
- _____
- _____
- _____

WHAT IS YOUR FAVORITE QUOTE?

- _____

And You Call This F-ing Leadership?

And You Call This F-ing Leadership?

Chapter 9

THE DARK DAYS GET EVEN DARKER

****

"If your conduct is determined solely by consideration of profit, you will arouse great resentment." - Confucius - Chinese teacher, editor and philosopher

On January 1, 2009, the general offices of FedEx Freight West were officially closed, and its operations combined with FedEx Freight East. With the merger of the two regional operations, The East and West designations were dropped and the company was renamed simply FedEx Freight. I will refer to FedEx Freight as FXF. This closing affected approximately 365 employees. As you recall, this group of employees were part of the first trucking company acquired by FedEx in the 1990's. This was also the group that had been promised for years that their headquarters would never close, nor would their operations ever be merged with that of American Freightways/FedEx Freight East. Yes, the times had changed, and the state of the economy could not have been predicted. This is why I am adamant about **Never promising employees that nothing is going to change. NEVER!**

While some of the displaced employees were offered positions in Harrison, only a handful relocated to Arkansas. The vice president of operations remained to head up the West coast service center operations that was now under the jurisdiction of FedEx Freight in Harrison. The president, who you'll recall came from FedEx Freight East, was transferred back to Harrison to assume the newly-created position of senior vice president of International Development. This position was created specifically for him and when he vacated the position, it was not backfilled. So, the American Freightways bias indeed protected the president of FedEx Freight West. The vice president general counsel was retained and operated out of an office located at a service center near San Jose to handle ongoing California-based litigation. As for the vp General Counsel being retained, it is best to simply state that our experience over the years proved that positions within the legal function appeared to be immune from any downsizing throughout the FedEx Freight segment.

Describing the closing of FedEx Freight West is important because we at FXNL (FedEx National LTL) very carefully watched how the entire process was handled, who was taken care of, who wasn't, etc. Many of us at FXNL believed that eventually we, in some way or the other, would face at least more significant downsizing, so the severance plan and the procedures put in place for handling the FedEx Freight West employees became very important. **REMEMBER, how displaced employees are treated during downsizings sends a critically important message to those employees who survive such downsizings.** Effective leaders should be as concerned about the emotions and perceptions of the employees who remain as they are about those being displaced.

On January 1, 2009, the U.S.-based salaried employees throughout the FedEx enterprise (all operating segments) had their salaries reduced by the amounts announced in the December 18, 2008 Earnings Release. No U.S. hourly employees at any of the operating segments received hourly pay reductions. In the case of FXF and FXNL, the hourly wage step progression's (usually based on years of service), top step was frozen, while the employees earning lower than top rate continued their wage pay progressions on their individual time tables. While many of the hourly employees did not take direct wage rate reductions, their working hours were reduced and the line-haul runs were reduced due to lower volume. Not reducing the wage rates of the hourly and mileage rated employees was a very calculated decision and primarily aimed at maintaining positive employee relations among the non-union, hourly ranks. The downside of this was the negative message it sent to all of the salaried employees. Many of the salaried employees felt that their pay was reduced because the corporation could get away with it without repercussions, especially from outside influences or groups. Almost every salaried employee understood the dire economic conditions across the country and simply sucked up their resentment about having their salaries reduced.

Most companies across the country, during this time period, took very drastic steps to reduce pay, eliminate incentive compensation plans and company contributions to retirement savings, reduce work schedules, layoff large segments of their workforces, etc. The country, the business community and most corporations were indeed in a fight for survival.

While on the topic of employees having to give up so much for the benefit of their companies' survival, I reflect on several of my philosophical beliefs. Through the decades, companies have marketed to their employees, their customers and the public-at-large that their success depended on their employees, that employees were essential to their growth, that their employees were the connection with their customers, etc. But, when the going gets tough for a company, the first response seems to be at the expense of the employees, the very group that makes superb customer service possible. While most companies will state that their largest controllable expense is their payroll, their leadership, by and large, often seems to talk out of both sides of their mouths.

I have always believed that the first things a company should do is to drastically cut all non-payroll type of expenses. Obvious measures are to curtail all travel except for trips essential to maintaining customer-facing interactions that build revenue. This includes unnecessary employee and management meetings, downgrading the hotels used during travel, limiting travel expense reimbursements for meals, etc. The list is endless if a management team wants to reduce their nonessential expenses. Only then can a management team look its employees in the eye and ask them to personally sacrifice for the sake of the entire organization. With that said, in my opinion, the pain of sacrifice should be shared with and felt by everyone at all levels.

It is important to note that, in the case of the U.S.-based FedEx enterprise-wide salaried employee pay reductions, the pay reductions were **never** reinstated. Those reductions became permanent. Once acceptable business levels returned and the profit goals were reaching normal expectation levels, the U.S.-based salaried workforce never regained the pay that had been taken during the recession's fight for survival. This reality was especially difficult to swallow as the FedEx race cars continued to run laps around the tracks of the NASCAR circuit. Yes, everyone understands the need for advertising and marketing, but not at the expense of the salaried employees who run the business and make the purchase of executive jets and race cars possible in the first place. As a life-long Human Resources professional, I simply think that speaks volumes. Sadly, in today's complicated and challenging business environment, many employees pass these things off by reflecting on their thankfulness to have a job, any job at any pay level. *And management wonders why employee engagement scores and loyalty indexes are at all time lows?* Current day **leaders must commit to protecting the employees they depend on to service their customers.** It's best to move on before my blood pressure increases again.

In early January 2009, FXNL announced and I quote from the bi-weekly Dispatcher: "In an ongoing effort to reduce costs, the decision has been made to phase out FedEx National LTL's free coffee, tea and hot chocolate service for the general offices, as well as the field. It may surprise you to know that this service costs more than $500,000 annually nationwide. While this is not a welcome change, we hope you understand the business logic of this decision."

That's right - the 75 plus years of company-sponsored coffee, tea and hot chocolate, was over. We transitioned to coin-operated hot drink machines and never looked back. The good thing, if there is a good thing, is that by this point, everyone knew how challenging the economy was and, if saving money on hot drinks could possibly help save jobs, then so be it. FXF had never sponsored hot drinks, so this pill was swallowed only by the FXNL workforce. I have always wondered if FXNL would have removed the hot drinks if FXF had provided hot drinks to its workforce. *Duh!* Some of our FXNL cynics believed that we lost company-sponsored hot drinks simply because

FXF never had it, just like the company cars and other tangibles. At the time, I personally believed the decision was a necessary business decision, and I drink coffee, tea and hot chocolate. But I also found the decision in keeping with my belief that desperate people do desperate things during desperate times.

On February 5, 2009, FedEx Freight initiated staffing adjustments affecting approximately 900 positions in about 130 facilities throughout the FedEx Freight network. This planned reduction was announced to management on December 12, 2008. These reductions were simply a reflection of the continued erosion of business levels and the need to better align the workforce with those business levels. Some affected employees were laid off, some were offered other positions in different service centers, and some had their hours reduced. In the short period since December of 2008, 1425 positions were affected throughout the FedEx Freight segment.

On March 19, 2009, FedEx announced its Third Quarter Earnings Release. The section reporting on the Freight segment stated:

"Less-than-truckload(LTL) average daily shipments decreased 13% year over year, as market share gains were more than offset by the worst LTL environment in decades. LTL yield declined 7%, due to lower fuel surcharges and the continuing effects of a competitive pricing environment resulting from excess capacity in the LTL industry."

"The operating loss reflects the extraordinary decline for freight services, the continued competitive pricing environment, costs related to the consolidation of our freight regional offices and severance charges from personnel reductions. These negative factors were partially offset by lower variable incentive compensation and continued stringent cost-containment initiatives, including the personnel and facility reductions."

For the entire FedEx Freight segment, revenue for the quarter was down 21%, the operating loss was $59 million, down from operating income of $46 million a year ago, and the operating margin of (6.5%), was down 4% from the previous year. One does not have to be a rocket scientist to know that things were about to get really ugly! The reality is - **Tough business environments demand tough decisions, because, at the end of the day, business always has been and always will be about making profits!** Never lose sight of this reality. Without profits, no company can survive long - profits are the fuel to corporate existence - pure and simple. Also realize that with this as the sole consideration, great resentment from the workforce is an equal reality.

On April 13, 2009, Bob Simons, our president and chief operating officer of FXNL, announced his "retirement" effective on May 31. Bob had almost 40 years in the transportation industry and was sad and hesitant about leaving, like many who must leave on other than their own terms. While Bob was of retirement age, he desired to work a few more years and had hoped to help FXNL finally reach its financial objectives before retiring. That expectation was out of his hands by this point in our distressed condition. The announcement of his "retirement" represented the second departure of a trusted and well respected FXNL president since our acquisition by FedEx.

At the time, while I suspected it, I was not aware that Bob's decision to retire was not his own because he was under a highly restrictive confidentiality agreement. I only discovered the facts a year later when I spent a week at Bob's bedside with him and his family before he passed away. He did however, unlike many, get to leave FXNL with his dignity and head held high.

In today's world, most officers at any publicly traded company realize that any day could be their last day. That reality simply goes with the job. And, as the public is well aware, many senior officers leave their jobs with rich severance packages, which the public simply accepts as an example of corporate excess and greed. While severance packages at FedEx Freight existed for all employee levels, none of them were by any means excessive or rich in comparison to many other corporations. I believe it is important to understand that **a severance package never makes the termination any less painful for the affected employee and his/her family.** A severance package for the custodian or the president of any company is just that, a cash offering in turn for an agreement to not sue the company - nothing more nothing less. As a manager, NEVER, let a severance agreement ease your conscience when terminating an employee - never. An employee termination should always bother you to some degree. When it no longer does, you have lost your soul.

While happy for Bob and his plans to relocate to Las Vegas, the workforce was now very concerned about who his replacement was going to be - an internal officer from within FXNL who they knew, respected and trusted, or someone from outside. Rumors abounded as they normally do when the president departs, regardless of the circumstances.

During May 2009, the FedEx Freight segment underwent another headcount reduction, but this one was primarily aimed at FXF System employees located in Memphis, Harrison and Lakeland. I vividly recall sitting with some FXF System managers in Lakeland, while they informed their employees of their separation. What made this whole process a nightmare was the affected employees' immediate forced departure from the building. We had to inform them that when they returned to their desks, they had to gather their keys and exit the premises and that their personal effects would be packed and delivered to their homes.

I had heard of this method of handling separations, but had never experienced it first hand. Nothing is more gut wrenching to employees than having to leave their work areas without even being able to say good bye to their coworkers, let alone the impact this has on the employees left behind. I repeat - **REMEMBER, how displaced employees are treated during downsizings sends a critically important message to those employees who survive such downsizings.** Effective leaders should be as concerned about the emotions and perceptions of the employees who remain, as those being displaced. Obviously, the FXNL employees who witnessed this process knew now, first hand, that any day they came to work could be their last. They watched their worst fears played out before their eyes.

Soon after Bob's departure at the end of May 2009, Jeff Baker, our senior vice president of operations at FXNL, received a call on a Thursday afternoon from the vice president of Human Resources at the FedEx Freight headquarters in Memphis. She informed him that if he wanted to be considered for the position of president, he needed to submit an application package to her office the coming Monday - yes, just three calendar days away. The package needed to contain a letter of interest, a resume and a PowerPoint presentation on what he would do during the first three months if he were selected for the position of president. *Really?* A man who had over 30 years of operations and sales responsibility with Watkins Motor Lines and a degree from Georgia Tech, now had to prepare a letter explaining why he wanted to be president, prepare a resume as if he were a stranger walking in off the street to apply for a position and develop a comprehensive presentation on what he would do during his first three months to address our business challenges. And all in just three days - two of them weekend days! He was also to do all of this on his own without help or assistance from anyone including his executive assistant. This was absolutely ridiculous and, in my opinion, at this executive level, absurd!

Well, Jeff worked non-stop to meet the deadline and mailed the extensive packet to Memphis on the following Monday, in time for it to arrive before the deadline the end of business that day. Soon after that, he was called to Memphis to formally "interview" for the position. He had a round of interviews with various senior officers and returned to Lakeland to await the decision while another candidate, not from FXNL, was being interviewed.

What still amazes me is how a multi-billion dollar corporation like FedEx Freight could handle such a senior position in this manner. The senior leadership clearly knew Jeff, knew his background and knew his capabilities. At the level of president at least, I believe all major corporations should have a very detailed and comprehensive succession plan that can be relied upon for replacing top senior level officers objectively and quickly. Not all agree with me on this, but it is a belief that I have held for years.

Within a short time of returning from Memphis, Jeff made a trip to Dallas for a Freight operations meeting. He was met at the airport by his boss, FedEx Freight's executive vice president of Operations who operated out of Harrison. He was informed that he would not be getting the position of president. Instead, FXNL's presidency would go to the senior vice president of International Development who was based in Harrison and who had been the president of FXF West. So, a person with just over 20 years of experience in trucking and no college education would be Jeff's new boss. Jeff was obviously shocked, deeply hurt and almost immobilized, so he skipped the planned meeting and immediately returned to Lakeland to await the official announcement. Simply put, Jeff felt terribly used and mislead throughout the whole process. It was now apparent to him that it had all had been a charade. Without saying, the senior staff close to Jeff was also shocked, but not surprised that the American Freightways bias had again won out as it had so many times since our acquisition. Most of us now believed that the FedEx Freight leadership simply wanted 'their man' in the position at FXNL and nothing else really mattered, especially given the economic times. Somehow they must have believed their candidate could perform miracles. As it played out, he, too, was unsuccessful in helping FXNL achieve its financial goals.

In my opinion, the leadership of FedEx Freight should have announced their choice for the position when Bob Simons "retired" and not have created the appearance of a charade. To most of us, including all the way thru our field operations hourly dockworkers and drivers, many of whom had known and worked with Jeff over the years, that's exactly what it was, a charade. Employees expect that senior leadership positions are filled through sophisticated succession planning processes, not a one time interview "show and tell" process. Handling it the way they did further eroded any remaining trust and integrity in the senior leadership of the Freight segment. To me, the right thing would have been for Freight leadership to tell Jeff, and our staff, that they were bringing in an outsider, one who had previously been an operating segment president, with the belief that a fresh new perspective and previous experience was critical at this juncture. That would have been, in my opinion, the most ethical way to handle the appointment.

****

"There is no such thing as a minor lapse of integrity." - *Tom Peters - author on business practices (In Search of Excellence)*

The FedEx Freight Communications Department in Memphis prepared the announcement, which was going to be sent simultaneously through a mass email distribution to the management of FedEx National LTL and FedEx Freight. This, in many ways, was going to be an extremely critical communication to our workforce. But, as bad luck would have it, we were told that there was a "glitch" in the email transmission and the FedEx Freight management team received the message long before our FXNL team did. FedEx Freight's field service center managers started calling ours and some of their general office managers started calling our general office with the news. When we realized that our entire company had been left off the announcement, we called Memphis and finally, 40 minutes after the Freight group were informed, our FXNL workforce was informed of who would be their new president and chief operating officer.

I am not making this up! This was an absolutely shameful execution of a very critical communication. Many at FXNL still believe that the email "glitch" was intentional by someone in the FedEx Freight Communications Department. How sad that our workforce had reached that level of distrust for the FedEx Freight organization and its leadership.

****

"Regardless of the changes in technology, the market for well-crafted messages will always have an audience." - Steve Burnett - founder of the Burnett Group

In mid-June of 2009, the new president arrived in Lakeland. He made the rounds talking with the officers and some of the key department managing directors. What I personally found alarming was that several friends and confidants on the FedEx Freight side called before his arrival to caution me to always be on guard, never to drop my guard, and to watch my back. I had not had to come to work feeling like that in literally decades - at least not since joining Watkins Motor Lines.

****

"Senior managers got to where they are by having been good at what they do.....so it's not surprising that they will keep implementing the same strategic and tactical moves that worked for them during the course of their careers.....I call this phenomenon the inertia of success. It is extremely dangerous." - Andy Grove - former COO, Chairman, and CEO of Intel Corporation

One of our new president's first directives was to move the 9 AM Monday morning staff meeting to 2 PM on Fridays. We had met every Monday morning since I joined Watkins in 1991. Frankly, most organizations meet on the first day of the week to discuss last week's results and plan for the current week. Oh well. We gathered at 2 PM on the first Friday and the meeting lasted until 6 PM. Most of us realized this was simply a power play to show us who was boss and to reinforce that we all needed to willingly fall in line. **One of the realities in work life is - the boss gets to be - the boss!**

Most of our staff meetings were spent with him holding court and treating us like we had never run a trucking company before. He loved nothing more than to lecture us on the various aspects of running a trucking operation or reviewing his stacks of mail aloud, sheet by sheet, while we listened and responded to his pontificating questions.

****

"Few people can see genius in someone who has offended them." - Robertson Davies - Canadian author, journalist and professor

During his eight-month tenure at FXNL he operated very independently of his direct staff. More often than not, he went around us to our respective staff groups for things he wanted done. He was far from a team player. I recall questioning my Human Resources manager about some employees who complained they did not receive their company birthday card, a tradition that had been in existence for decades. She said that my new boss had told her to not reorder when the supply ran out because they were no longer wanted by the employees. She naturally assumed that he and I had discussed it. When I questioned my boss about it he said rather curtly that he had decided there was no longer a need for the birthday cards. No discussion, no dialogue, not even a heads up that he had decided to cancel a 75-year old cultural tradition. As trivial as this may sound, it is offered as one small example of our new president's management style.

Never forget, one must respect the rank or position - the rank holder must personally earn the respect and trust that the rank or position represents.

****

"Trust cannot thrive in an environment where we preach teamwork and cooperation, but seldom recognize or reward it." - Wayne R. Bills - president and founder of the Personal Effectiveness Institute

The primary thing I do believe the new president of FXNL did right was work with us to prepare a very detailed plan that would greatly reduce our line haul costs by shifting more freight to rail. The downside was that it would require longer delivery times. He was passionate about this plan and believed it would make a major difference in our long-term strategy of being a low-cost long-haul carrier within the FedEx Freight segment. He presented it to the staff at FedEx Freight in Memphis, but it was rejected by the Marketing Department. He returned to Lakeland very dejected - welcome to our world, one we had grown accustomed to during the previous three years.

On June 17, 2009, FedEx announced its Fourth Quarter Earnings Release. The section on the Freight segment reported more grim statistics. Revenue for the quarter was down 28% from last year, the operating loss was $106 million, down from operating income of $99 million a year ago, and the operating margin was down (11.2%), down from 7.6% the previous year. We obviously were deteriorating from bad to worse with no light at the end of the tunnel. FXNL was continuing to miss its financial objectives as was the entire Freight segment.

In August of 2009, it was announced that the entire FedEx Freight System Information Technology group, the Sales group and the Pricing group would be reassigned to the long established FedEx Services segment. This would bring all IT, Sales and Pricing under one unified management group. This made perfect sense from a business standpoint and, while long overdue, was a real sign to many that the FedEx enterprise and its management teams would bring the absolute best oversight and practices to a centralized team of professionals serving the greater good of FedEx overall, and FedEx Freight in particular. The problem of each operating segment essentially doing their own thing with their own self serving interests would be ending. Some within the Freight segment expressed that this would not necessarily be good because there would be a loss of control over these groups. *Hogwash!* The time was far overdue to end the self- serving perspective of these groups operating separately. I was finally beginning to gain some respect for FedEx because very positive steps were being taken to start breaking down the many barriers and silos that existed.

As the Freight System employees began realigning to FedEx Services, new problems emerged. For the most part, the benefits and pay structures of the FXF and FXNL employees since our acquisition in 2006 had become very similar if not identical. FedEx Services had different levels of benefits, benefit premium contributions, retirement plans, vacation benefits, etc. It took some time for the employees in both segments to accept these differences as a new reality in their work life. Again, having a job was better than griping about benefit and pay differences.

It did, however, become a running joke. For example, two married employees driving to work together in the same car going to the same building, one wearing a FedEx Freight ID badge and one wearing a FedEx Services ID badge, had different pay scales and benefit packages. As further illustration, the same years of company service would grant higher vacation benefits to a FedEx Services employee, so one spouse could have four weeks of vacation while the other had five weeks despite having the same years of service. Frankly, I never got used to this disparity, but learned to finally accept it. If the employees could tolerate it, then why shouldn't I? **Every battle is not worth fighting.** In today's reality, one must carefully pick the battles they are passionate about and then devote full energy to those that will make a difference for both the employees and the business.

On September 17, 2009, FedEx announced its First Quarter Earnings Release. The portion on the FedEx Freight Segment explained that revenue of $982 million for the quarter was down 27%, the operating income was $2 million, down 98% from $89 million a year ago, while the operating margin was 0.2%, down from 6.6% the previous year. While the economy was still struggling and we continued to face many challenges in the market place, to many of us at FXNL, these numbers were, in some ways, a sign that maybe, just maybe, the uphill climb had begun.

Then, on September 23, 2009, the FedEx Freight president and chief operating officer, based in Memphis announced his retirement to be effective in February 2010. WOW! In most corporations, this is huge news and usually comes as a surprise, as this did. So now the big question in all our minds - who will replace him? Over the past three years, we at FXNL had grown very accustomed to the American Freightways bias affecting almost every major decision within the FXF segment, so why should this be any different?

The rumors were endless and we simply had to wait until FedEx Corporate made a decision and announced it. The other big question was what would 2010 hold for FXNL? Could the days get any darker? Would the new leader and president of the FedEx Freight segment finally stop the endless and senseless change and financial bleeding? Would the ongoing effects of inadequate leadership finally end?

****

"A new leader has to be able to change an organization that is dreamless, soulless and visionless....someone's got to make a wake up call." - Warren Bennis - scholar, author and organizational consultant

MY CHAPTER 9 - LEADERSHIP "AHA'S"

****

- **NEVER** promise employees that nothing is going to change.
- **REMEMBER**, how displaced employees are treated during downsizings sends a critically important message to those employees who survive such downsizings.
- Tough business environments demand tough decisions, because at the end of the day, business always has been and always will be about making profits!
- One of the realities in work life is - the boss gets to be - the boss!
- Never forget, one must respect the rank or position - the rank holder must personally earn the respect and trust that the rank or position represents.
- Every battle is not worth fighting.
- Truthful and straight forward communication is always respected by employees - don't manipulate employees, they see through it.
- Regardless of a severance package, it cannot sooth the emotional and psychological pain and damage of being terminated or cast out.

WHAT ARE YOUR CHAPTER 9 "AHA'S?"

- _____
- _____
- _____
- _____

WHAT IS YOUR FAVORITE QUOTE?

- _____

And You Call This F-ing Leadership?

Chapter 10

THE DAWN OF A NEW ERA

****

"The true mark of a leader is the willingness to stick with a bold course of action - an unconventional business strategy, a unique product-development roadmap, a controversial marketing campaign - even as the rest of the world wonders why you're not marching in step with the status quo. In other words, real leaders are happy to zig while others zag. They understand that in an era of hyper-competition and non-stop disruption, the only way to stand out from the crowd is to stand for something special." - Bill Taylor - co-founder and editor of Fast Company magazine and former editor of Harvard Business Review

Just before Thanksgiving 2009, it was announced that the new FedEx Freight president and chief operating officer, headquartered in Memphis, would be coming from the FedEx Express segment. The person selected had 20 years with FedEx and was the executive vice president & chief operating officer over the FedEx Express world wide flight and U.S. domestic ground operations. While cautiously optimistic, there was never a happier group than most of us at FXNL. To many of us, this was hopefully the dawn of a new era - it gave us hope that our dark days might be ending.

It seemed that the new FXF president was, in our opinion at least, appointed to the Freight segment to stop the financial bleeding and to return the segment to profitability. He had long-term proven leadership abilities and was highly respected by the FedEx world-wide workforce. Anyone we came across who had worked with or around him couldn't speak highly enough of his leadership strengths, his integrity, and his excellent communication skills. A FedEx Express employee told me how lucky we were to get our new president and how sad they were to be losing him. That spoke volumes! Indeed, the new president had his work cut out for him.

On December 17, 2009, FedEx announced its Second Quarter Earnings Release. The portion on the FedEx Freight Segment explained that revenue of $1.07 billion for the quarter was down 11%, the operating loss was $12 million, down from operating income of $32 million a year earlier, while the operating margin of (1.1%) was down from 2.7% the previous year. The economy was still very much a tremendous challenge, unlike anything seen previously by anyone during their working careers.

Shortly before the earnings release date, I was contacted to attend a short, yet highly confidential meeting to be held in Memphis on December 18, 2009. As my wife had learned since FedEx entered our lives, everything to do with FedEx Freight seemed to be highly confidential, but this meeting seemed especially secretive. I slipped out of Lakeland under the pretense of having a quick HR meeting in Memphis.

A small group of 18, representing such key functional areas as HR, IT, Operations, Legal, Marketing, etc., gathered in the FedEx Freight Headquarters conference room. The new segment president started the meeting by having all of us sign a nondisclosure confidentiality agreement which, once signed, bound us to keep the project highly confidential or risk being terminated. I thought, oh no, here we go again!

The new president asked our committee to return for the first full working session in early January to begin developing a comprehensive action plan to combine the operations of FedEx Freight and FedEx National LTL into one company, which was to be effective in June. His vision was to have the freight segment operate both a regional and long-haul operation from the same service centers using one workforce and dual utilized equipment. Wow! You could literally hear a pin drop in the room. Most sat there in utter amazement and disbelief. Some expressed their concerns that essentially reflected long-held beliefs in the industry that a company could not effectively serve both the regional markets and long-haul markets from the same facilities. I reminded the group that Watkins Motor Lines had both regional and long-haul services operating out of the same terminals in about half of the company's locations when FedEx acquired it. The group reacted as if I had not spoken a single word - except for a few glares from around the table, which was not a surprise. The new president patiently listened to everyone and then simply, but firmly, stated that our task was to make it happen by June, no excuses. He emphasized his belief that our committee represented the best talent in the industry, so the task was indeed possible.

****

"The very essence of leadership is that you have to have vision. You can't blow an uncertain trumpet." - Theodore M. Hesburgh - president emeritus of the University of Notre Dame

What a flight back to Lakeland! My head was spinning with the cold reality that what we at FXNL had feared for so long was now officially the decision to merge the two entities. The more deeply I thought about a merger the more it made total sense from a business perspective. The reality was that the company I had worked for since 1991 no longer existed. FedEx Freight had stripped it of almost anything resembling what Watkins had been. Our long-haul network had been gutted and replaced with a regional model, we had eliminated a number of perks, killed the recognition programs and family picnics, replaced bonus plans with smaller ones, lowered salary grades, changed titles, changed staffing models, had closed service centers, relocated and disrupted or terminated literally thousands of employees, and had never achieved our financial objectives since the day we were acquired, despite having been profitable for almost 75 years before hand. Furthermore, our long established employee culture no longer existed, it was simply a spiritless and dead organization. So, what realistically was the last step in a bungled acquisition, but to finish it off and combine the operations. The very sad reality was that the days of FedEx National LTL were now very limited, and my job was to facilitate the merger, or in other words, extermination, to the best of my ability. So, for what most of us thought was the dawn of a new era with the new president, turned out to be the pending sunset of an old era that had a proud and rich history of entrepreneurial growth and success.

****

"The only way to make sense out of change is to plunge into it, move with it and join the dance." - Alan Watts - British philosopher, writer and speaker

When the Christmas holidays were over, the merger committee reconvened in Memphis. Several members of the committee had developed realistic reasons why more time was needed to pull all of the pieces together - example, all the software programming that was required, the dock and line haul freight flow planning, the development of new manpower staffing models, etc. The new president, however, was steadfast in his goal to implement this merger in June - just five months away. In an effort to meet this deadline, the core committee started quickly adding new subject matter experts from across the various FedEx segment of companies.

****

"We are continually faced with a series of great opportunities brilliantly disguised as insolvable problems." - John W. Gardner - former president of the Carnegie Corporation of New York

Unlike what had been done with the Watkins acquisition, the new FXF president reached across multiple operating segments of FedEx and engaged highly competent key employees including top staff officers from the FedEx corporate office to assist us in the planning process. I often found myself wondering what might have become of the FXNL organization if that many talented people had been engaged in making the Watkins acquisition as successful as this merger was mandated to be. At least one thing was clear - this project had the best of the best engaged in doing it right - and all without any American Freightways bias. To me, this was indeed a new era.

****

"The most essential factor is persistence - the determination never to allow your energy or enthusiasm to be dampened by the discouragement that must inevitably come." - James Whitcomb Riley - American writer, poet and author

The day-to-day operations of both companies continued on while behind the scenes the confidential merger teams worked frantically to meet the June deadline. Nothing seems to drain one's energy more than the demands of a highly sensitive, confidential project while trying to maintain, on the surface at least, the air of *business as usual*. Eventually, those around you begin to smell the scent of change in the air and the bonds of trust begin to slowly erode.

In February 2010, the president of FedEx National LTL, who had come from FXF/American Freightways, resigned and left the company, just eight months after relocating to Lakeland from Harrison. He told us that he could not shut down another company as he had done with FedEx Freight West. Most of us did not buy his story since we believed that most rational senior executives don't leave a key officer position without either another job or a severance package - neither of which he had. His departure was not troubling in the least to most of us at FXNL. For the first time in months, we didn't have to come to work everyday looking over our shoulders. Nothing erodes the fabric of an organization more than distrust in the leadership.

****

"Age wrinkles the body; quitting wrinkles the soul." - Douglas MacArthur - General of the U.S. Army

On February 19, 2010, the new FXF president in Memphis announced the following organizational change and I quote: "I am pleased to announce that Jeff Baker, senior vice president of Operations, will assume management responsibility for FedEx National LTL, effective immediately. Jeff will report directly to the executive vice president and chief operating officer, resulting in the elimination of the position of president and ceo, FedEx National LTL. This change supports my commitment to better align and streamline the functionality of the Freight segment for improved efficiency." So, after being informed just eight months earlier that he was not qualified to be the president of FXNL, Jeff was finally the leader of FXNL. How ironic! By then Jeff was aware of the plans to shut FXNL down and merge the operations with those of Freight. He entered his new role with a very heavy heart indeed. Rumors were beginning to surface about "the super secret project" and this announcement only fueled more rumors and anxiety. Not much could have been done to quell the rumors at that point.

The many merger committees continued to work feverishly on such things as, the process to dovetail the hourly workforce, how to handle the salaried workforce, how to re-engineer the docks for freight flow and realign the line haul networks across the country. The endless hours of conference calls and secret meetings seemed to increase as the months passed more quickly than we liked. Finally, the reality of so many key events having to occur within such a short time frame resulted in the decision to delay implementation of the organizational transitions until late summer of 2010. While this was good news indeed, that meant prolonging the secrecy and the growing anxiety among the workforce.

On March 18, 2010, FedEx announced its Third Quarter Earnings Release. The portion on the FedEx Freight Segment stated as follows:

"Less-than-truckload (LTL) average daily shipments increased 26% and LTL yield declined 8% year over year due to the effects of discounted pricing. Operating loss increased in the quarter due to lower yields and higher purchased transportation costs."

While the revenue was up 14% from last year, the operating loss was $107 million compared to an operating loss of $59 million a year earlier, and the operating margin of (10.3%) compared to (6.5%) the previous year. Yup, the sins of the past had finally caught up with the FedEx Freight segment. During the really ugly times of the recession, FedEx Freight, like many in the trucking industry, drove pricing down to almost ridiculous levels just to get freight on the trucks which kept their operations running through cash flow. I vividly recall that with one major customer, every $1.00 we earned in revenue, it took us almost $1.40 in operating costs to service it. It doesn't take an above average intelligence to figure out that short-term decisions made during tough economic times would eventually catch up with a company. One might ask, *what were they thinking?* However, such pricing decisions seem so well-founded when made in the heat of a battle for survival. Many trucking companies in the industry were facing similar consequences. I was simply surprised that FedEx was not above those levels of desperation - being so short-termed in their approach.

In April of 2010, the FXNL vice president of operations and the managing director of the Southern Region Operations, both originally from American Freightways, resigned. We then realigned our operations management group to avoid having to replace these two positions since we knew the merger would eliminate them anyway.

During the spring of that year, I was brought under yet another non-disclosure agreement regarding an outside consulting firm that would be evaluating the overall staff structure of the entire FedEx Freight segment. This project was running in tandem with the merger project, so it wasn't too difficult to see that big changes would be coming to the entire Freight segment. No one really knew from one day to the next what the future would hold. We simply learned to come in each day, do our best to stay focused and positive. The reality was - big changes were long overdue and ultimately, regardless of the hardships the changes were going to inflict, the segment very much needed a complete overhaul.

Well, you no doubt saw this coming. In early May 2010, my position as vice president of Human Resources at FXNL was eliminated as was the vice president of Human Resources at FedEx Freight in Harrison. The vice president controller at both FXNL and FedEx Freight in Harrison were also eliminated as were the positions of vice president, general council at both FXNL and FedEx Freight in Harrison. The president of FedEx Freight in Harrison announced his retirement, effective June 1, so that position was also eliminated.

As the communication announcement to management stated, these position eliminations were a result of the transformation of several nation-wide staff support functions moving from a decentralized operating company-centric design, to a matrix model, with centralized leadership based at the FedEx Freight Corporate Headquarters in Memphis. This affected incumbents holding those positions, except for the two officers in the legal departments who retained their titles of vice president, but changed reporting from their respective operating companies to the senior vice president, general counsel at the FedEx Freight headquarters in Memphis. The Human Resources and Financial functions also changed from reporting to their operating unit presidents to the respective functional vice president at the headquarters in Memphis. Finally! The FedEx Freight segment had just one president and one group of staff officers overseeing the entire segment. It was about time and way overdue, and, while painful to see more employees go out the door, the result was one that should have been achieved much earlier in our assimilation into the FedEx organization.

I was one of the lucky ones since I was offered the position of managing director of Human Resources over the FXNL Human Resources function, now reporting directly to the vice president of Human Resources in Memphis. My counterpart in Harrison was not so lucky since the managing director of HR position there was occupied. I was lucky in that my managing director of HR had stepped down a year earlier to assume a vacated senior hr manager position in the field and we did not backfill his position. Had we backfilled it, I would have been terminated in May 2010. Since I was not ready to retire and was in the middle of the merger project, I was very glad to turn down my severance package and accept this demotion. What a fluke of fate - a decision I made a year earlier not to backfill a position is the only reason I survived this reorganization.

****

"When fate hands you a lemon, make lemonade." - Dale Carnegie - American writer and lecturer

Looking back at all the reorganizations, re-engineerings, the closing of FedEx Freight West, the staff reductions, job eliminations, the realignments, the Legal Department seemed to be the only one that escaped totally unharmed. While this created resentment among many staff members, I do admire what can occur when the top leadership of a function stand up for their people and their function. On the people side of business, one will often come across things that do not seem fair. In the end, **strong leaders who try to do the best for their people are the winners**. One cannot fault reality, even if it does seem unfair at the time.

****

"It is better to have a lion at the head of an army of sheep, than a sheep at the head of an army of lions." - Daniel Defoe - English writer, journalist and author

On June 16, 2010, FedEx announced its Fourth Quarter Earnings Release. The portion on the FedEx Freight Segment stated as follows:

"Less-than-truckload (LTL) average daily shipments increased 34% and

LTL yield declined 6% year over year due to the effects of discounted pricing. Operating losses in the quarter were driven by lower yields and higher volume-related costs, as significantly higher shipment levels required increased purchased transportation and other expenses. The quarter's operating loss also reflects an $18 million impairment charge related to the goodwill associated with the acquisition of Watkins Motor Lines (now FedEx National LTL). Last year's results included $100 million of charges, mostly related to impairment of goodwill associated with the acquisition of Watkins Motor Lines."

The revenue was up 30% from last year, the operating loss was down to $36 million compared to an operating loss of $106 million a year ago, and the operating margin of (2.9%) had improved compared to (11.2%) the previous year. Yup, the sins of desperate pricing strategies continued to plague the segment, not to mention the costs associated with writing off more of the Watkins acquisition investment. Just maybe, the merger of the two companies and the continued strong leadership emerging in Memphis would result in a long-term sustainable operating segment. Just maybe. **And just maybe, had the acquisition been better planned and executed there wouldn't have been a write-off at all……just maybe.**

On July 20, 2010, I received a letter from the FedEx Freight president informing me I had been selected as one of the FedEx Freight Five Star Award winners for that fiscal year. The Five Star Award is the most prestigious form of recognition given to any FedEx salaried employee. Individuals must exemplify superior leadership, creativity and efforts in support of FedEx's external and internal customers in order to receive the award. While difficult to get excited about receiving an award that, in many ways, represented my committee work to shut down and merge FXNL, I was humbled that the new president recognized my leadership and contributions.

I have come to realize that many leaders have to get involved with very difficult and highly unpleasant projects throughout their careers such as downsizings, mergers, layoffs, etc. The key is to do what the organization expects to be done, like it or not. **I have always believed that as long as my boss didn't ask me to do something that was illegal, unethical, or immoral, then I needed to do it to the best of my ability.**

The confidential merger committee, which now numbered

between 2,000 and 3,000 employees across the entire FedEx organization, was working at an almost indescribable pace in preparation for the announcement, now scheduled for sometime in September. The intensity was almost exhausting. Nerves were wearing thin and having to maintain confidentiality continually kept everyone on pins and needles. Finally, the date of the announcement was closing in. While a relief on one hand to see it finally coming together, we all deeply dreaded it.

****

"Nothing in this world can take the place of persistence. Talent will not; nothing is more common than unsuccessful men with talent. Genius will not; unrewarded genius is almost a proverb. Education will not; the world is full of educated derelicts. Persistence and determination alone are omnipotent." - Calvin Coolidge - 30th President of the United States

On Thursday, September, 16, 2010, also the day of the FedEx Corporation first quarter earnings release, it was announced that FedEx National LTL would close on January 30, 2011 and combine operations with FedEx Freight. This closing would shut down the Lakeland FXNL Headquarters complex affecting 175 employees, as well as, close approximately 100 FXNL facilities across the country with the layoff of about 1700 employees. The Lakeland downtown building devoted to FedEx Services employees (former Watkins Motor Lines employees) was not affected by this announced closing.

I will never forget Jeff Baker and I making that announcement to our Lakeland employees along with our other two FXNL officers. Looking out at the group I saw employees who had 20, 25, 30+ years of devoted service to the company. The pained expressions, the tears, the realization that all their hard work and efforts to making FXNL a success, had now culminated in nothing but a severance package, if they stayed until the closing date. The highway that had been paved with so many promises, hopes and dreams just four years earlier by FedEx Freight was now littered with broken promises and the fear of the unknown. Our employees faced entering the worst job market in the worst economy in their working careers. The announcement had essentially the same impact at all the FXNL facilities across the country. At this point, the employees knew they were occupying property that would soon be closed and their individual fates had yet to emerge. While the announcement had finally been made, I deeply dreaded the next four months as we faced the task of shutting down a 75-year-old company and combining the operations and some of our employees into FedEx Freight.

****

"Every single time you make a merger, somebody is losing his identity. And saying something different is just rubbish." - Carlos Ghosen - chairman and CEO of the Renault-Nissan Alliance

I could almost write a separate book about the four grueling months that followed the announcement. After the initial shock had sunk into the workforce, the process of communicating the specific impact on each employee began. The hourly employees in the field, would, for the most part, be dovetailed into the FXF workforce. This meant that the combined hourly workforce would be ranked according to their seniority date at each remaining facility. Obviously, the FedEx Freight workforce was furious over this dovetailing procedure because our employees, for the most part, had more seniority than their FXF counterparts.

The complicated part of this process was closing 100 FXNL facilities, and moving that planned freight flow over to the FXF facilities, and then staffing each with sufficient employees to service their respective customers. Alignment of the hourly dovetailed workforce into the existing FXF facilities, as well as the 25 FXNL facilities that were remaining open, was an almost impossible task. But, eventually, after months of meetings and talks with every affected hourly employee, the task was concluded and everyone knew where they were going and what job they would have beginning in February.

As for the FXNL salaried workforce, that was a different story. The decision had been made that no salaried employee would be bumped from a job by a more senior salaried employee holding the same job at a closing facility. Also, the decision was made that the existing salaried staff at each facility would remain in place, which meant that most of the salaried employees at FXNL facilities that were closing would be terminated, unless they could bid on and qualify for a vacant salaried position within FedEx Freight, before the merger. What upset me and many others was, for example, that our operations managers were one salary grade lower than FXF operations managers and were not, therefore, eligible for vacancies that might occur prior to the merger. So, in the end, most of the FXNL Region, District, and Service Center salaried staff were not able to blend into the FXF operation when the merger was concluded. Both hourly and salaried employees within the Lakeland FXNL headquarters were not able to bump or dovetail into comparable jobs at FXF. Less than 25 of the Lakeland based FXNL employees ended up accepting offers for vacant positions in Harrison. Many of the FXNL field salaried staff of Human Resources, Engineering, etc., did move over to FXF and maintain their jobs following the merger. Nothing was simple during this excruciating and complicated process. Again, an entire separate book could be devoted to this very burdensome merger process for the FXNL salaried employees. Many are still bitter to this day over not being able to secure a position with FedEx Freight that they were indeed qualified for. Others who were nearing retirement age and were assigned positions at FXF, were bitter when their offers to take the severance so that another, younger employee who needed and wanted a job could have theirs, were rejected as "exceptions not in the rules." To force someone in their 60's to work who wanted a severance makes no absolutely no sense.

During the four months leading to the merger, Jeff Baker and I traveled to various FXNL service centers. It was clear that there was no energy left anywhere in the company. Most of the people seemed like dead folks walking. While many would end up having a job at FXF, many did not look forward to their new life with a group of employees who had shunned them on customers docks and in interactions between the two groups just a few years earlier. The hard cold reality was quickly setting in - having a job was "probably" - - "maybe" - - better than having to be on the street during these economic times. For those who faced being on the street, there was true fear and panic. Everyone knew that their severance payments would run out quickly.

The months for many at FXNL were filled with cleaning out files and disposing of years of records, pictures, memorabilia, and preparing the equipment for transfer to FXF, while still servicing customers. The facilities had to be prepared to close and the support vendors on almost anything you can imagine like beverage vending, trash removal, cleaning services, etc., had to be notified of the contract terminations. Some days it felt as though I was attending a number of funerals while other days were just dull and gray. The Thanksgiving and Christmas holidays were very difficult, as you can imagine. The workplace celebrations had a very dismal undercurrent while many employees were questioning if they'd have jobs before the next year's holiday season. These times were filled with deep personal anxiety and true fear of the unknown.

To help those who would lose their jobs we were able to offer employees at our large facilities onsite career counseling through a national outplacement consulting firm. Employees at smaller facilities were able to access counseling services over the telephone. These outplacement services helped employees prepare resumes or job history sheets, think about and prepare for conducting a job search, interviews, and the whole process of moving on to a new life outside of FXNL. Along with the outplacement services, all affected employees were informed what their severance payouts would be and the requirement that they sign severance agreements which are promises to not sue the company or speak or write badly of it. These agreements also required an acknowledgment that the employee could never again ever work for any FedEx company. Some employees, who were able to obtain employment, chose to leave before the merger, but most stayed so they could earn what their company tenure entitled them to. **REMEMBER, regardless of the amount received in a severance package, it cannot soothe the emotional and psychological pain and damage of being terminated or cast out. No amount of money can erase rejection.**

Obviously, many of our employees would have jobs at FedEx Freight after the merger. The city and line haul drivers as well as many office clerical employees would be dovetailing into FXF facilities along with our maintenance shop technicians. Some salaried employees were able to qualify for openings. And about 25 of the FXNL facilities in the field would remain open after the merger. At our Lakeland Headquarters, the vp of Transportation and Maintenance would be relocating to Harrison as a vice president. Our legal vice president would be relocating to Memphis along with me as a managing director of HR Administration. Jeff Baker was retained in an office in Lakeland for an additional six months to help coordinate the shut-down of 100 National facilities across the country. How sad, I thought at the time, the very guy who wasn't selected to be president of the company he spent 30+ years building, could now shut it down. But on the positive side, it was six months of additional employment for him. We had three others relocate from Lakeland to Memphis and about 15 or so Line Haul Dispatch employees relocated to Harrison. So in the end, between 1,200 to 1,800 employees lost their jobs due to the merger and received severance payouts in return for signing severance contracts agreeing not to sue FedEx.

The end of January 2011 came faster than we had thought possible given the dread of closing. The last two weeks at the Lakeland headquarters were just miserable. Closing down offices, emptying desks, boxing up files to send to Harrison, throwing out anything that wasn't needed in Harrison. The same occurred in the 100 field locations where the grief over Lakeland closing compounded the fields own grief and anxiety over having to move to a new FXF facility. Many of the field employees and managers had years of relationships, even if just developed over the phone with headquarters employees and managers, and they, too, were losing "family."

Two weeks before our official closing, all the vending machines were pulled from the Lakeland FXNL buildings. While we complained, we were told that the vendor jumped the gun, which most of our employees believed was actually one final shot from the Harrison group. Little things like this mean so much during times of personal stress for employees. **Effective leadership ensures that all the small details in downsizing environments are planned for and executed properly and compassionately.** The devil is in the details.

During the last two weeks of January, many departments finished their final tasks, and the employees started to dwindle throughout the complex. Some departments were totally empty by the time our last day arrived. We in Human Resources needed to finalize the shipping of files and records, so we had to work right up to the last lonely day. On Friday, January 28, 2011, I met my Lakeland-based department at the time clock at 4:45p.m. in the Human Resources area. We all stood together as each one clocked out for the very last time as an employee of FedEx National LTL. Some in the group had worked together for decades. I had been with the group since 1991. We all hugged and walked out the door together with tears streaming down our faces, arm in arm. We got in our cars and drove around the complex several times honking our horns and then exited the driveway - looking in our rear view mirrors for the last time to say good bye to FedEx and FXNL. I was one of the few lucky ones, I got to start a new job on Monday in Memphis. Most in my department faced a very scary and uncertain future while I walked out with a very heavy heart filled with survivor's guilt.

What happened to the Watkins Motor Lines and FedEx National LTL workforce should not have happened. The four years at FedEx National LTL was a gut wrenching journey down a corporate highway that proved to be a devastating dead end for thousands of employees thanks to the combination of a weak economy and inadequate leadership. One can only imagine the total cost in dollars for this bungled acquisition, let alone the long-term effects on the impacted employees and their families. Simply put, FedEx Freight failed to deliver either the long-haul system, the value proposition or the "pent up demand" it had promised the FedEx Corporation.

****

"When small men attempt great enterprises, they always end by reducing them to the level of their mediocrity." - Napoleon Bonaparte - French military and political leader

What was I going to discover about FedEx through my new assignment in Memphis? Would the leadership be more competent than I had experienced during my first years with FedEx Freight? Would I eventually come to appreciate the widely held reputation of FedEx for being a world class organization and great place to work? Could I regain my trust in large publicly-held corporations? Would I regret not taking my severance package and ending my career with the closing of FXNL?

MY CHAPTER 10 - LEADERSHIP "AHA'S"

****

- Leaders must embrace change, regardless of its negative consequences. Change is essential for long-term survival.
- Key projects demand the talents of the best people. Never accept less and always demand full commitment from the team.
- One can not over-plan or over-prepare for key change projects.
- As much as an organization attempts to minimize the negative effects of change on employees, the human toll will linger long after the change has occurred.
- Severance payments can never diminish the sense of loss nor the effects on the family of impacted employees - never.
- Too many highly confidential projects rust the bonds of trust between all employees.
- Caring leaders offer downsized employees much needed career counseling and outplacement services. Also, remember that how displaced employees are treated during downsizings sends a critically important message to those employees who survive such downsizings.

WHAT ARE YOUR CHAPTER 10 "AHA'S?"

- _____
- _____
- _____
- _____

WHAT IS YOUR FAVORITE QUOTE?

- _____

And You Call This F-ing Leadership?

And You Call This F-ing Leadership?

Chapter 11

DISCOVERING THE REAL FEDEX

****

"I have always been delighted at the prospect of a new day, a fresh try, one more start, with perhaps a bit of magic waiting somewhere behind the morning." - *J.B. Priestly - English novelist, playwright and broadcaster*

On Monday morning, January 31, 2011, I started my new job as the managing director of Human Resources Administration at the FedEx Freight segment headquarters in Memphis. I felt lucky and terrible all at the same time. Lucky, because at 66 I still had a job (I was not ready to retire and the economy was still struggling), and terrible because the previous Friday we closed the doors on FedEx National LTL and I had to say goodbye to so many long-time friends whose futures were tenuous at best. I very much needed to gather my wits and enter this new job with renewed enthusiasm.

****

"Every new beginning comes from some other beginnings end." - *Seneca - Roman Philosopher*

In my new position I reported to the segment's vice president of Human Resources. I was responsible for employee compensation and benefits, Human Resources Development, the Human Resources Information System and all of the Human Resources administration and administrative services for FedEx Freight's 32,000 employees. I had a staff of five in Memphis and approximately fifty in Harrison. The segment headquarters in Memphis had fewer than fifty employees, and I must admit, the atmosphere was very different from what I had expected. No one's ego seemed inflated, nor did anyone seem to be on a power trip. Everyone was friendly, cooperative and respectful of each others' schedules and project demands. In short, it was a very quiet even-paced professional environment, where everyone was very serious about returning the FedEx Freight segment to profitability.

****

"We must always change, renew, rejuvenate ourselves, otherwise we harden."
- *Johann Wolfgang von Goethe - German writer and politician*

Since many of us in Memphis supervised segment employees who were based in Harrison, we routinely traveled there to oversee and coordinate workflow. For the most part, I found the Harrison employees cooperative and pleasant to work with – the air of superiority that those of us from FXNL had encountered early in our merger relationship, seemed to have diminished. There was a notable transition from interfacing with them in 2006 to interacting with them in 2011. Most realized they had survived those very tumultuous years – the shut-down of FedEx Freight West, the shut-down of FedEx National LTL, the overall segment downsizing, the departure of some long-term leaders – and were just glad that they had a job.

I realized early on that if I was going to be successful in directing my Harrison groups, I had to create a level of trust and establish myself as their new leader, and not the guy from FXNL who carried any perceived baggage. I worked very hard to accomplish both of those goals and I think I was successful. In the year-and-a-half that I worked with them, I believe that they understood I was serious about my job, but at the same time we had fun working together. My time getting to know them and working with them also helped me to lose some of the bitterness I had developed watching the dismantling of FedEx National LTL.

And You Call This F-ing Leadership?

****

"A sense of humor is part of the art of leadership, of getting along with people, of getting things done." - Dwight D. Eisenhower - 34th president of the United States

On March 17, 2011, FedEx announced its Third Quarter Earnings Release. The portion on the FedEx Freight Segment stated as follows:

"Less-than-truckload (LTL) yield increased 11% primarily due to yield management initiatives. LTL average daily shipments decreased 6% as a result of the yield management initiatives and the severe winter weather.

On January 30, 2011, FedEx Freight and FedEx National LTL combined operations, launching a new unified LTL freight network that offers customers the choice of two levels of service - FedEx Freight Priority and FedEx Freight Economy - from a single company. As a result of this combination, the segment incurred one-time costs of $43 million during the quarter and $130 million fiscal year-to-date due primarily to lease termination costs and severance expenses.

The operating loss in the quarter included the costs associated with the combination of the FedEx Freight and FedEx National LTL operations. Severe winter weather also significantly impacted results. The segment benefited from one additional operating day during the quarter."

And so it was, after a $780 million acquisition and literally millions and millions and millions of dollars in losses, write-offs and merger costs, the chapter on the Watkins Motor Lines asset acquisition was finally closed. May all of the wonderful memories live on and the lessons it provided us on leadership never be forgotten.

As the new president's leadership style and philosophy took hold in the segment, there was a discernible power shift from Harrison to Memphis. While the American Freightways bias was still present, it played less and less of a role in the day-to-day operations of the back-office functions. However, the bias continued relatively unchecked in the field operations. Now that there was only one president for the entire FedEx Freight segment, it made the shift to traditional management control easier. From my perspective, the Harrison employees are now being influenced much more by the "real" FedEx culture; however, there is still an undercurrent of the American Freightways bias and the shift to a 100% FedEx culture will take some more time. In addition, as long as there are segment officers based in Harrison who are influenced by the American Freightways bias, it will probably always be, in my opinion, a house divided between the Memphis group and the Harrison group.

****

"Organizational culture is the sum of values and rituals which serve as 'glue' to integrate the members of the organization." - Richard Perrin - author and management consultant

Before June 2011, Jeff Baker, nearing the completion of his post FXNL assignment, was offered another six-month extension that would expire in December of that year. Jeff had just spent six months overseeing the closing of 100 facilities across the country including the Lakeland headquarters complex on Griffin Road. He had also worked on the operational merger of FedEx Freight and FedEx National LTL. He was very disappointed that FedEx Freight did not offer him a permanent position as had been done for the president of FedEx Freight West, when that company was shut down and merged into the operations of FXF. For that person, they created a new officer position to protect his employment status. As Jeff told me, he was simply tired of being used, so he turned down the six month extension and took his severance package. Immediately after leaving FedEx Freight, he became the president of a company in the Watkins Trucking Group, working again for Chip Watkins.

****

"Always recognize that human individuals are ends, and do not use them as means to your end." - Immanuel Kant - a German philosopher and author

Watkins Motor Lines alumni were saddened to learn of the passing of John Watkins on August 23, 2011. That was also the same day that Jeff Baker was diagnosed with terminal cancer and given only a few months to live. I had the opportunity of talking with Jeff almost every day during his remaining time. He maintained such an incredible strength during those final weeks, and for many, set an example on how we all should face our last days with humor, reflection, grace and dignity. He asked me to say a few words at his funeral to which I agreed on the condition that he write his final speech and I would read it to those gathered. Jeff died on October 10, 2011, at the age of 61. The words of his last speech are now on a permanent plaque in the Watkins Conference Room of the Harrison office complex, where there is a separate conference room dedicated to each of the three companies that comprised FedEx Freight. The Watkins Conference Room has old photos and memorabilia from Watkins Motor Lines. Jeff exemplified the true character of a senior leader. In my opinion, he was one of the key leaders who played an instrumental role in helping the entire Watkins workforce smoothly and quickly transition to FXNL. To help ease their anxiety, his favorite expression when addressing employee meetings in those earlier years was "we have married up."

****

"Leaders must encourage their organizations to dance to forms of music yet to be heard." - Warren G. Bennis - American scholar, organizational consultant and author

On our return flight to Memphis from Jeff's funeral, my wife asked when I was going to finally retire and enjoy some quality time while we both had our health. As she pointed out, Bob Simons had passed away in April 2010 at age 69, John Watkins at 71 and now Jeff Baker at 61. Some of the officers I had spent years with at Watkins had also died over the last three years. So, after pondering the reality of her question, I promised I would pick a date before the end of the year.

****

"The harder you work, the harder it is to surrender." - Vince Lombardi - head coach for the Green Bay Packers

During the months that followed, I was very busy with various projects that enabled me to interact with employees at segments outside of FedEx Freight. I was so relieved to find them to be what I had always envisioned about FedEx. There is probably no more committed, professional, compassionate, and energized workforce than what I found at FedEx. I was finally able to truly appreciate why FedEx is recognized around the world for being a great place to work. I often thought how sad it was that our FXNL workforce didn't have the opportunity to meet the same quality workforce that I had. The FedEx workforce has every right to be proud of their organization for they are the real FedEx. The real FedEx is a first-class organization that exemplifies what leadership can accomplish through a very trusting relationship with its workforce.

****

"The supreme quality for leadership is unquestionably integrity. Without it, no real success is possible, no matter whether it is on a section gang, a football field, in an Army, or in an office." - Dwight D. Eisenhower - 34th President of the United States and Supreme Allied Commander during WWII.

On January 16, 2012, my 67th birthday, I announced my retirement effective in June. While my original intentions had been to work a few more years, the time had come to move on, while still in good health, and enjoy whatever years I had left. After 43 years in Human Resources management, it was indeed my time to retire.

****

"If people concentrated on the really important things in life, there'd be a shortage of fishing poles." - Doug Larson - columnist and editor

The last six months in Memphis were the most rewarding. I continued to travel weekly to work with my Harrison groups, worked in Memphis on ongoing projects, and participated in the fiscal year end planning, budget preparations for the new fiscal year, etc. It was during this time that the idea of writing a book on leadership hit home with me. What Al Lucia (referenced in my Acknowledgements) had told me years earlier was true - that when I was passionate enough about a subject, I'd want to write about it. The revelation that FXNL had been demolished through, primarily, inadequate leadership, was well worth my time in retirement to write about. My title seemed to eloquently describe my feelings about what we all had gone through together.

****

"Age is only a number, a cipher for the records. A man can't retire his experience. He must use it." - Bernard Baruch - financier, statesman and political consultant

I have been asked several times if I thought the merger of the two organizations was worth the costs, the countless hours of work, and the impact on thousands of employees' lives. I believe the earnings release on March 22, 2012, for the third quarter, helps to position my opinion on that. The results for the third quarter for the FedEx Freight segment were:

- *Revenue of $1.23 billion, up 10% from last year's $1.12 billion*

- *Operating loss of $1 million, compared with an operating loss of $110 million a year ago*
- *Operating margin of (0.1%), up from (9.8%) the previous year*

"Less-than-truckload (LTL) yield increased 6% due to higher LTL fuel surcharges and base yield improvement. LTL average daily shipments increased 2% reflecting sequential improvement during the quarter and favorable comparisons due to severe winter weather in the prior year.

The operating results in the quarter improved significantly as a result of the positive impacts from higher yield and volume, milder winter weather, one additional business day, and ongoing improvements in operational efficiencies. In the prior year quarter, the segment incurred one-time costs of $43 million due to the January 30, 2011 combination of the FedEx Freight and FedEx National LTL operations."

My short answer would be a "qualified yes," but only after one accepts that FXNL realistically no longer existed in any shape or form. FedEx Freight had stripped it of almost anything resembling the company they acquired in 2006. Of critical importance in any business scenario, FXNL had never achieved its financial objectives due, in my opinion, to accounting, sales and economic circumstances largely beyond our control. So, FXNL had transmogrified into a spiritless, dead and unprofitable organization. In the final analysis, merging the two organizations was the only alternative. Worth it? Depends on whose side you stand - the side of the stockholders, the side of the company, or the side of the employees. I believe that all three sides were seriously shortchanged throughout the four years that FXNL existed. I don't believe now is the time to question the decision to merge, but only to face the reality that - **"It Is What It Is!"**

Now that the dust has settled and the marketing and pricing of the two service products have been embraced by the marketplace, the FedEx Freight segment has returned to profitability and has joined the FedEx's worldwide reputation as a dependable transportation carrier. The employees who survived all the turmoil of the merger can now work and fully focus on delivering the "Purple Promise" which is the collective commitment to make every FedEx experience outstanding.

And You Call This F-ing Leadership?

****

"Well, you would have to say what is the criteria to determine the success of any merger? It would have to be that the companies are stronger financially, that they took market share, and they are on a very steady footing in terms of their performance." - Kevin Rollins - former president and CEO of Dell

In writing this chronicle: the case study of a 75-year-old successful company succumbing to the effects of inadequate leadership and a bad economy, I have tried to show how not to lead while also providing many examples of good leadership. I have tried to be factual in the presentation of the story and in laying out examples of both good and inadequate leadership and their effects on a workforce. But, there are still some unanswered take aways on leadership. In essence, it is now time to share my personal advice or perspectives on the key principles or points of being an effective leader. These points of leadership, which are described in Chapter 12, have guided me throughout my entire career.

****

"The essence of a successful business is really quite simple. It is your ability to offer a product or service that people will pay for at a price sufficiently above your costs, thereby giving you a profit that enables you to buy and to offer more products and services." - Brian Tracy - author and motivational speaker

MY CHAPTER 11 - LEADERSHIP "AHA'S"

****

- Recognize that survival guilt is a real consequence in downsized workforces.
- A leader must build trust in each new assignment with new employee groups. Trust is not carried from job to job. It is earned with each move.
- The use of humor is essential in building trust and breaking down barriers.
- Most employees simply want to do a good job, be recognized and appreciated for the work they do.
- Leaders must recognize and respect company cultures.
- The decision to retire is difficult and complex. Don't assume that age alone eases the decision making process or acceptance to do so.

WHAT ARE YOUR CHAPTER 11 "AHA'S?"

- _____
- _____
- _____
- _____

WHAT IS YOUR FAVORITE QUOTE?

- _____

And You Call This F-ing Leadership?

Chapter 12

THE POINTS OF LEADERSHIP

****

"The most dangerous leadership myth is that leaders are born - that there is a genetic factor to leadership. This myth asserts that people simply either have certain charismatic qualities or not. That's nonsense; in fact, the apposite is true. Leaders are made rather than born." - Warren G. Bennis - *American scholar, organizational consultant and author*

In this, my last chapter, I will try to summarize my overall concept of effective leadership and give you a limited summary of what is certainly a very complex and exhaustive subject. To grasp just how exhaustive, conduct a search on "leadership" and you'll find no less than 100,000 different book titles on the subject, plus endless lists of CD's, DVD's, blogs, websites, etc. Obviously, this one chapter cannot do it justice, nor is it intended to. I do hope, however, that this chapter will entice you to begin researching and studying more on your own; particularly as you reflect back on the case study you just read about the disastrous effects of inadequate leadership. Because of that I think it is important for us to close by looking, even briefly, at what characterizes effective leadership and ask ourselves how we can emulate those traits so that our actions as leaders have a positive impact on the employees we supervise and the organization that employ us.

Now, I am not an academic nor a famous executive who can command an audience interested in my perspective on leadership; however, I have learned throughout my career that leaders are not born, they are made through years of education, training, coaching, mentoring and learning. Learning can be through formal education, on the job training, certifications, apprenticeships, etc. But nothing teaches the difference between leadership theory and reality better than being in the trenches and learning from mistakes. Becoming an effective leader requires a life-long pursuit of the best practices and methods of highly successful leaders and then applying those learned practices. It is also critical to ask yourself periodically - **"Am I the leader for whom I would want to work?"**

Over the last 100 years, there have been many theories or approaches to leadership. For example, there are alternative theories, the trait theory, attribute and style, positive reinforcement, situational and contingency, functional, integrated psychological, transactional and transformational, the leader-member exchange, the neo-emergent theory......and the list goes on and on. Eventually, all of these converged in recent times to two basic theories - trait and process.

The trait theory can best be summarized by "He is a born leader" which supports the school of thought that people are born with the qualities necessary to lead. This theory asserted that leaders, for example, were smarter, more confident, and more insightful. This theory was reinforced by the belief that most leaders had similar critical characteristics or drives - as in a drive for responsibility, self-confidence, ability to influence, determination, etc. In short, the trait theory focused on the personality characteristics of the leader. This theory began eroding in the late 1940's and 1950's when some academics began questioning why this theory failed to consider situational factors affecting leadership. In other words, they questioned why some people never became leaders who had the requisite personality characteristics.

A more popular theory today is the style theory, which emphasizes a leader's behavior and how he/she acts in order to attain their leadership in certain situations. The style theory views leadership as a process of learned behaviors that enable the leader to interact with a group of followers in a given environment to achieve a goal. This theory of supports and reinforces the need for ongoing training and development in leadership skills so the leader will know how and under what environment to apply the process necessary to seek adaptive and constructive change in achieving the organization's goals.

Leaders exercise their influence over their followers through various leadership styles. I believe one should understand the most common core leadership styles so they can identify which style is being used or is dominant at any given time by a leader. This analysis will help determine which style is a good fit for the given circumstances and challenges.

For purposes of this chapter, I have narrowed the list to the six that I personally have preferred to identify with through the years. and that I have admired in others. My choices do not make them necessarily the right ones nor are they all inclusive. They are just my personal favorites. I challenge you to develop your favorite list after doing some reading and research into this ever challenging - and changing topic.

My favorite six leadership styles are:

#1. The **autocratic leader** (come with me) keeps close control over followers through adherence to policies and procedures given to the group.

#2. The **transactional leader** (follow the rules) focuses their leadership on motivating followers through a system of rewards and punishments.

#3. The **transformational leader** (change agents) works to change or transform his followers' needs and redirect their thinking - they challenge and inspire their followers with a sense of purpose.

#4. The **democratic leader** (what do you think) shares the decision-making process with followers by promoting the interests of the group and by practicing social equality.

#5. The **laissez-faire leader** (hands off, leave it be) gives the followers all the rights and power to make decisions.

#6. The **paternalistic leader** (father knows best) takes care of their followers, as a parent would his/her children, by showing deep concern for them.

These leadership theories, styles and methods are not complicated. The first step is understanding them. The second step is learning when and how to use them or any combination of them. Also, one style or method does not fit all circumstances or all employee groups. Most leaders tend to "lead" with one style - their first or preferred style, then employ others as required or needed. The art of effective leadership, in my opinion, is to assess a situation and then employ the leadership style that will ensure that all the followers join together to accomplish the needed change. It's really that simple.

In writing this case study, I was going to point out some of the various leadership styles that I admired and those I found ineffective. Frankly, no one label can fit a leader all the time. For example, the founder of Watkins Motor Lines was clearly a very autocratic leader in the formative years of Watkins. As the company grew he shifted to more of a transactional leader, but he often reverted back to being very autocratic depending on the business challenge. Indeed, no one leader can effectively maintain the same leadership style. The exceptions to this are those leaders who specialize in a particular style and move from company to company where that particular skill set is in demand at the time. Once they accomplish the required change process, they move on to the next company.

So, what exactly is leadership? A very simplistic definition is that leadership is a process of social influence in which one person enlists the assistance of others to accomplish common goals or tasks. To do this effectively takes a commitment to study the art of leadership and develop your own preferred approach to leading. An excellent book which balances theory with a practical approach is written by a professor of communications at Western Michigan University, Peter Northhouse, entitled, "Leadership: Theory and Practice." Another superb and easy to read book from a very practical standpoint is written by my friend, Al Lucia, entitled "The Street Savvy Leader." Both are available on Amazon. **Make the pursuit of learning** about leadership one of your career goals and commit to it.

Another important step is to **start and maintain a "Leadership Journal."** You can start this at any point during your career journey - the key is starting and maintaining it until you retire. Start by thinking of every boss you have had and write down their names and what you admired about their leadership styles and, equally important, what you didn't like. Remember, we learn just as much by discovering what we don't want to emulate as we do from what we admire. Develop these lists, and soon you will see patterns emerge. As you continue to read and research the subject of leadership, write down the key lessons that resonate with you. Write down your favorite leadership quotes and leadership "AHA's." Your "Leadership Journal" should be a working document that you read from time to time for self-motivation and inspiration on how you can be an effective leader - all learned behaviors from those who have gone before you.

Not long ago I was asked what things I learned along the way that I felt were fundamental for me as I developed into a leader. What was the glue that seemed to bond together all the lessons I had learned. For me, the most fundamental lessons or the glue that has connected all of my experiences and education goes back to my youth when I was a very active Boy Scout. While becoming an Eagle Scout and earning Vigil Honor in the Order of the Arrow (the BSA national honor society), I must have repeated the 12 points of the Scout Law thousands of times. Those 12 points became my foundation. While I can also point to my military training and experience and the countless role models I worked for and with over my career, all roads lead back to my experiences as a Boy Scout.

In writing this case study, I realized that I could explain these 12 points in business terms, and that they may serve as a helpful guide to others in their quest for improving leadership skills and becoming good role models. Obviously, one doesn't have to have been a Boy Scout to be an effective leader. But, most successful leaders, both men and women, have lived their careers following these same guiding principles, whether they realized it or not.

In 1908, the founder of the Boy Scout Association, British General Robert Baden-Powell, wrote the Scout Law. He drew inspiration from the work of Ernest Thompson Seton, who founded

The League of Woodcraft Indians (an American youth program) in 1902 and later became instrumental in spreading Scouting throughout North America. Baden-Powell chose to use a set of affirmative laws in contrast to Old Testament-like prohibitions. He also drew inspiration for the Scout Law from the Bushido code of the Japanese Samurai, the laws of honor of the American Indians, the code of chivalry of European knights, and the Zulu fighters he had himself fought against. These laws were written for Scouts everywhere, not just in Britain and were modified over time in keeping with text appropriate for each country.

The Scout Law is a mission statement of sorts for all scouters, young and old. It is the defining principle that binds the organization together. It is simple, direct and yet compelling and certainly timeless. I have come to realize that these 12 principles are as valid today and in today's business environment as they were when they were first written for young boys more than 100 years ago. These principles are as applicable for women as they are for men. If only we could have all the leaders around the world live by these core values, if only all of our business leaders would live by them as well.

The 12 points of the Scout Law, or as I like to refer to them in today's business context, **The Points of Leadership,** are: A leader must be Trustworthy, Loyal, Helpful, Friendly, Courteous, Kind, Obedient, Cheerful, Thrifty, Brave, Clean and Reverent. Let me define what I believe is the meaning of each of these from the perspective of today's business environment. A leader is:

#1 - TRUSTWORTHY

A trustworthy leader is a person whom you can rely upon. He is true to his word and can be counted on to follow through on commitments. Throughout this book I have discussed the meaning and value of trust in an organization's leaders. To me, trust is the fundamental core value upon which everything in leadership rests. Without trust, nothing can be sustained long term. Everything a leader represents starts and ends with the core principle of trust. Effective leaders keep their promises.

****

"Trust is the lubrication that makes it possible for organizations to work." - Warren G. Bennis - American scholar, organizational consultant and author

#2 - LOYAL

A loyal leader will have your back at all times and will never betray that which he believes in. I believe that effective leaders must first be loyal to their profession - be it accounting, marketing, legal, human resources, quality control, operations, whatever. They should abide by the professional standards and code of ethics of their profession. Second, they should be loyal to their organization. It is the organization that expects, respects and supports their loyalty to their professional standards. In turn, the organization has the obligation to expect loyalty from its employees. Loyalty down earns loyalty up, it is not a one-way proposition. Third, effective leaders should be loyal to both their employees and their immediate superior.

****

"I can't expect loyalty from an army if I don't give it." - George C. Marshall - American military general and Secretary of State

#3 - HELPFUL

A helpful leader does his best to make life easier for others and to ensure that their working environment is the best it can be. Helping can be providing tools, whenever possible, for your employees to perform to the best of their ability. Helping can be as simple as taking the time to listen to an employee's problems and offering support and guidance. Helping can be nothing more than showing you care, offering a helping hand, mentoring an employee new to a different role, helping a peer who needs some advice on a particular issue. Being helpful means making people around you know that you care more about them than you care about putting your own interests first.

****

"We can't help everyone, but everyone can help someone." - Dr. Loretta Scott - author

#4 - FRIENDLY

Friendly leaders make others feel comfortable and welcome in any situation. Friendly leaders smile, use humor to lighten the mood, are approachable, and work hard at making employees feel they care about them and consider them equal in every way. Everyone knows and understands organizational hierarchy and most respect titles and managerial status, so there is no reason to be pretentious or arrogant or unfriendly. Friendly leaders make it a habit to get to know as much about their followers as possible - their kid's names, their hobbies, and their interests. Friendly leaders also share something about themselves - about their families, their hobbies, their interests, as well as sharing life's issues like births, deaths, graduations, etc. Friendly leaders ask their followers for their opinions on how the organization could be improved. Unfriendly leaders are not effective in the long run.

****

"I forgot to shake hands and be friendly. It was an important lesson about leadership." - Lee Iacocca - *American businessman, president and CEO of Chrysler Corporation*

These first four Points of Leadership really describe *what kind of person* an effective leader should be - Trustworthy, Loyal, Helpful and Friendly. The next four Points of Leadership describe how an effective leader *should act* - Courteous, Kind, Obedient and Cheerful.

#5 - COURTEOUS

Courteous leaders show respect for others and put others ahead of themselves. They always mind their manners. They listen carefully before interjecting their views. They allow everyone their time and turn to express their opinions, and they never demean or embarrass their followers.

****

"Don't flatter yourself that friendship authorizes you to say disagreeable things to your intimates. The nearer you come into relation with a person, the more necessary do tact and courtesy become." - Oliver Wendall Holmes - *Associate Justice of the U.S. Supreme Court*

#6 - KIND

Effective leaders are kind to others and display a caring attitude. They always go out of their way to be nice to their fellow employees. They respect all employees at all levels of the organization and treat everyone as equals. Kindness can be as simple as a passing smile in the hall, a kind greeting, looking into the person's eyes when they are talking to you, being mentally present when they are talking to you, extending simple human kindness. Effective leaders live the axiom of treating others in the same way as they themselves want to be treated. In our hurried times with our demanding schedules, we sometimes sacrifice kindness for expediency. Who doesn't want to work for a leader who is kind?

****

"There is no need for temples, no need for complicated philosophies. My brain and my heart are my temples; my philosophy is kindness." - Dalai Lama - a high lama in the Gelug school of Tibetan Buddhism

#7 - OBEDIENT

Effective leaders follow the rules - - all of the rules all of the time. Every profession has rules or codes which they expect their professionals to follow. Every organization has rules - rules on treating customers and each other, rules on following an endless list of local, state and federal laws under which we all must operate, etc. When we break the rules or laws or codes, we can no longer be effective leaders. Effective leaders can not expect employees to act obediently if they don't set the same example. I also believe these rules extend to our personal lives with our families, as well as, our community lives. Effective leaders do not pick and choose what rules they will follow and which ones they will ignore. Nothing can justify not following the rules.

****

"Obedience of the law is demanded; not asked as a favor." - Theodore Roosevelt - 26th president of the United States

#8 - CHEERFUL

Effective leaders are positive role models for their organizations. They go through life with a positive attitude and in a positive manner. People do not work effectively in a negative environment nor for leaders who always seem to be down about things. While I'll give any leader one down day here and there, followers look for leaders who inspire, who are confident, who embody enthusiasm and "a positive can do" attitude. It is not always easy to maintain a cheerful demeanor, but that comes with the territory of being an effective leader.

****

"Cheerfulness is the atmosphere in which all things thrive." - Jean Paul Richter - German novelist and humorist

Of the 12 Points of Leadership, the last four points describe how an effective leader *should lead his or her life* - being Thrifty, Brave, Clean and Reverent.

#9 - THRIFTY

Effective leaders do not waste corporate resources and highly value the guidelines that budgets represent in the daily operation of the enterprise. They do not spend carelessly because they have the power or authority to do so. Leaders have the responsibility to be a caretaker of the company assets, with a fiduciary responsibility to safe guard and manage the assets well. Ask yourself if you would be comfortable seeing your expense report published on the front page of your local newspaper. Effective leaders do not support an entitlement mentality when spending organizational resources - be it travel, ordering office equipment and supplies, organizing recognition or appreciation functions, etc. All eyes in an organization see leaders who do not value the organization's resources.

****

"Waste is worse than loss. The time is coming when every person who lays claim to ability will keep the question of waste before him constantly. The scope of thrift is limitless." - Thomas A. Edison - American inventor and businessman

#10 - BRAVE

Most associate the term "brave" with acts of valor. In my opinion, in a organizational setting, it means living according to the commonly accepted standards, both personal, and those associated with the profession. This means sticking with the straight and narrow when those around you want you to stray from what you know is right. Many of us can name corporations that have been charged with accounting irregularities, for example, because their leaders deviated from what they knew were the right principles or laws. It takes guts, or bravery to go against unscrupulous leaders. It also takes guts to stand up for employees or at least to be willing to express your concerns when facing the negative impact of potentially poor organizational decisions. Effective leaders must be brave.

****

"Success is not final, failure is not fatal: it is the courage to continue that counts." - Winston Churchill - British Prime Minister

#11 - CLEAN

The general term of "cleanliness" has long been one of our society's key virtues. In the context of leadership, I believe the characteristic of being clean relates to caring for our health and honoring our body and our mind. Effective leaders monitor their physical well-being and maintain a routine fitness regimen so they are always physically fit and up to the demands of long work days and the pressures associated with today's business environment. Effective leaders also keep a sound mind through getting enough rest and having activities and interests outside of the business environment that helps them recharge and stay alert and fresh. Effective leaders take their authorized vacation time and holidays and expect and encourage their employees to do the same.

****

"Take care of your body. It's the only place you have to live." - Jim Rohn - American entrepreneur, author and motivational speaker

#12 - REVERENT

Reverence can be a delicate topic in some organizations. However, I do believe that most of us have been exposed to some form of spirituality through our formative years. Being reverent is being respectful. I believe, in the context of leadership, effective leaders must respect the religious beliefs of others, which includes having a working knowledge of the beliefs and practices of the world's major religions. Regardless of your personal beliefs, to deeply respect and support the religious beliefs of your employees will be very meaningful in your continuing quest to grow as an effective leader.

****

"Affirmation of life is the spiritual act by which man ceases to live unreflectively and begins to devote himself to his life with reverence, in order to raise it to its true value." - Albert Schweitzer - German physician, philosopher and theologian

In addition to embracing the Points of Leadership and pursing the requisite leadership education and training, leaders must also be competent in their particular field. Competence is the critical attribute that completes the total leadership package and it leads to earning your followers' respect. As most will agree, it is very difficult to respect a leader who is not competent. Effective leaders also must have intense focus and drive, as well as the willingness to sacrifice other pursuits. While most leaders do not possess every ideal attribute, they do, however, know how to compensate for their shortcomings. And at the end of the day, effective leaders simply work hard, if not harder that their followers. When you have competence, hard work and respect, coupled with a high level of trust, it's amazing what an effective leader can accomplish.

My own particular views on leadership have been molded through 40-plus years of on-the-job experience, education, learning and observing. I have worked for a variety of leaders – some excellent, others mediocre and some down right ineffective. And I have come to realize that the biggest mistake some leaders make is to allow arrogance, manipulation, self-indulgence, greed and entitlement to occupy the space in their minds that is needed to foster effective leadership habits.

So, one last time, in summary, what is leadership? It is the process of social influence in which one person induces the help of others to accomplish common tasks or goals. The methods used to elicit followers to follow depend on the leader's personal style, as well as the urgency of the situation and challenges of the work environment.

****

"Leadership is the art of getting someone else to do something you want done because he wants to do it." - Dwight D. Eisenhower - 34th President of the United States Chairman of the Joint Chiefs of Staff

Hopefully, by now you are assessing your own leadership strengths and weaknesses and are beginning to reach a higher level of leadership awareness. My key overall message to you is simple. If you are interested in improving your leadership skills, then you must make a serious commitment to the study of leadership. Seek out a mentor who you can dialogue with on best practices. Read leadership books, both academic, as well as, practical. Read the articles published by highly successful leaders from industry, government and the military. **Maintain a Leadership Journal.** Last, be willing to take risks and make mistakes along your path. Get feedback by asking your followers how you are doing. Nothing teaches better than the bitter taste of hard-earned experience. Good decisions come from wisdom. Wisdom comes from experience. Experience comes from making bad decisions and learning from them.

In writing this case study, I chronicled four years of countless examples of both good and inadequate leadership. I have also provided a variety of leadership quotes that represent various leaders and people from different occupations and countries. There is a price for inadequate leadership that often results in a detrimental and negative effect on the lives of thousands of employees and their families. Let the many mistakes, missteps, oversights and shortcomings that occurred during the demise of FedEx National LTL be a reminder and a challenge to you to be the best leader you can possibly be. Routinely ask yourself, **"Am I the leader for whom I would want to work?"**

****

"How are you doing as a leader? The answer is how are the people you lead doing? Do they learn? Do they visit customers? Do they manage conflict? Do they initiate change? Are they growing and getting promoted? You won't remember when you retire what you did in the first quarter or the third. What you'll remember is how many people you developed - how many people you helped have a better career because of your interest and your dedication to their development. When confused as to how you're doing as a leader, find out how the people you lead are doing. You'll know the answer." - Larry Bossidy, CEO, AlliedSignal

RETROSPECTIVE

A RETROSPECTIVE OF WATKINS MOTOR LINES THROUGH THE EYES OF THE EMPLOYEES.

During the summer of 2006, just prior to the closing of the acquisition, Watkins published a twelve page magazine entitled "Our history and your thoughts." The first two pages provided a history of notable firsts for Watkins Motor Lines. The remaining ten pages contained thoughts from the employees. When the communications department asked our employees for their memories of Watkins Motor Lines and their thoughts on the future of becoming FedEx National LTL, we received many heartfelt submissions. I would like to end this book by quoting some of those thoughts while leaving off the names of the employees who submitted them. These are examples of the team spirit that was fostered by good leaders.

"I can remember the day I got a phone call offering me a job at Watkins. I was so excited to have an opportunity to work for a company that I had heard so many great things about. Mostly, I was grateful that I was going to be able to provide for myself and my young son. The day the phone call came, it changed our lives." - 6 year employee from the Lakeland Receivables Management Group

And You Call This F-ing Leadership?

"I am thankful and appreciative to have been part of a great company. When I would mention Watkins as my employer, people would say, 'I've heard that's a good company to work for.' I've met and have grown to know many wonderful people (some who remained and other who have moved on) who played a part in my learning experiences and growth. Even through economic times, Watkins showed commitment to employees' well-being by maintaining its workforce - that's caring. One of my most memorable thoughts was the company picnic at Mary Holland Park in Bartow, FL. My daughter was eight months old (she is now 22) when she tasted her first ice cream bar. She screamed and cried for more; John Watkins was standing next to us and said, 'Good Lord, what's the matter with her?' I said, 'ice cream…' and before I could finish the sentence, John ran over to the nearby cooler saying, 'Let's get that kid some ice cream.' It worked and we were all laughing about it because it shut her up. Picnics were the time when you relaxed and got to know your co-workers and the owners. Thanks, Watkins family, for allowing me to be a part of your growth and giving me the chance I asked for 32 years ago. I wish you the best for the future." - 32 year supervisor from the Lakeland Receivables Management Group.

"I had only worked for Watkins about nine days and was given a delivery to my former employer, C.P. Brown (Brown Transport). The shipment was driver collect so I had to go in and get a check. When I walked in I was sent to Mr. Brown's office and he and another gentleman were sitting there. He asked where I was working and I told him Watkins. He started asking about Bill Watkins (the founder), if he was a tyrant or a tight wad. I said that I didn't know, that I had never met him and C.P. said, 'Let me introduce you,' and the other guy was Bill Watkins. After getting a check and thanking Mr. Brown, I borrowed the phone to call the dispatcher and was told to take my lunch. When I said I was going to lunch they asked me to join them. I had been with the company less than two weeks and had lunch with the chairman of the board." - 16 year city driver from Atlanta, GA.

"We were at the National Truck Driving Championship in New Orleans. We had just eaten a great meal at The Redfish Grill. Clay Watkins, myself and several others were standing on the sidewalk when Clay pulled out a can of Copenhagen and we both got a dip of snuff. Where else could you share a chew of tobacco with the company vice president but Watkins!" - 7 year city driver from Knoxville, TN.

"If memory serves me correctly it was the late 70's that the independent truckers went on strike; and for safety reasons, Watkins decided to run in convoys lead by (employees from) the Safety Department. One leaves on the West Coast and the other leaves on the East Coast and low and behold they both arrive at

our one bay shop in Fort Worth at about the same time. We had trucks lined out our driveway down the street across the bridge and down the freeway in both directions from east and west. Needless to say the local police showed up and said to get these trucks off the road or they will start issuing tickets. And at the time there were only two of us on duty. We did comply and get all off the highway." - *30 year trailer mechanic from Dallas, TX*

"I'll never forget a meeting I attended downtown when I was in Accounts Receivable. One of the speakers was Steve Newhouse. He was a riot and he had me laughing so hard I was crying. It was then I realized that you can work for a living, but have fun doing it. Thank you Steve. I will never forget your enthusiasm, I am sure you will do for FedEx what you did for Watkins." - *9 years sales employee from Lakeland, FL*

"In the short five years I have been with Watkins there have been so many changes/improvements. We do not even look the same. That is even more true now with FedEx. My best memory of Watkins is how easy it was to communicate to upper management, how genuine they were. At Madison we are all one family....could not ask for a nicer bunch of people to work for!" - *5 year account executive from Madison, WI*

"I have enjoyed my time at Watkins. I started as a casual filing clerk and worked on the switchboard and in Customer Service. I went full time in 1988. It always thrills me to see Watkins trucks on the road and also seeing them roll in and out of the gates. I also enjoyed receiving birthday and anniversary cards signed by the Watkins family." - *18 year OS&D clerk from Charlotte, NC*

"Watkins has been a great company to work for because of the people we work with. Everyone's attitude and dedication is contagious in a positive way. I look forward to another 10, 20, 30+ years with all of you. The family culture is what made Watkins what it is today. And a huge benefit in the future for FedEx National LTL." - *9 year equipment control supervisor from Salt Lake City, UT*

"I am proud to have been a part of WML for 23 years. Watkins has always been respected in the transportation industry and their ethics and equipment has certainly proven that. Company pride and customer satisfaction have always been my goals. Commitment and integrity is not what you do, but who you are. I'm sorry to see the end of an era with Watkins, but I am looking forward to working with FedEx National LTL - continuing to strive for excellence." - *23 year city driver from Nashville, TN*

"I have truly enjoyed my time with Watkins Motor Lines. I was treated like a real person, not a number. All managers and dispatchers were the best. I'm *glad I came to work at Watkins. Hope FedEx will be as good or better." - 1+ year line haul driver from Oklahoma City, OK*

"Watkins was the best company I have ever work for. They were good to me and my family. I will always appreciate what they did for me." - 26 year city driver from Opelika, AL

"Three weeks into my career with WML I had to attend a Southern Regional meeting. This was held in the conference room on Griffin Road. At that time, the Southern Region consisted of seven terminals; 15 account executives and terminal managers were in attendance and I was the only female. I was very intimidated, but quickly became Watkinized. I have always felt since that meeting that I was 'one of the guys,' and was treated that way. What a great group of folks!" - 19 year account executive from Tampa, FL

"About two weeks after being hired John Watkins came into my office to chat - I was nervous and looking for something intelligent to say. We were on the third floor looking down into the Lakeland terminal yard, and I noticed a vendor washing one of our units. So I, being the new guy wanting to impress John said, 'Mr. Watkins, I understand we spend $1.5 million a year washing our equipment and that means we have to generate about $1.5 million in revenue to cover that cost.....so why do we spend so much to clean them?' John got up, had me stand next to him gazing out of the window looking at the washing and he put his arm on my shoulder and said, in his deep southern drawl, '....if your name was on the side of the truck, you'd want em clean too!' I then proceeded to attempt to get both of my feet out of my mouth." - 15 year sales officer from Lakeland, FL

"I have always appreciated and enjoyed the many extra perks the company has provided, especially during Employee & Contractor Appreciation Week, where there was never a day without a special event. Thanksgiving was a warm celebration, which brings everyone together as one big family and, and then there's cubicle decoration and Toffee Coffee at Christmas. All of the holidays were so enjoyable with everyone's ingenuity and clever creations bringing so much joy to all! I still laugh at Dick and Linda in the Hawaiian costumes serenading all. Each year they had a different idea. Also, I especially enjoyed the company picnic with great food, entertainment and lots of fun and laughter with not only fellow co-workers, but with family as well." - 17 year employee from Lakeland receivables management group.

****

"Teamwork is what the Green Bay Packers were all about. They didn't do it for the individual glory. They did it because they loved one another." - *Vince Lombardi - head coach of the Green Bay Packers*

THE END

****

"If I read a book that cost me $20 and I get one good idea, I've gotten one of the greatest bargains of all time." - *Tom Peters - American writer on business practices*

ABOUT THE AUTHOR

Steven H. Newhouse is a retired vice president and managing director of Human Resources from FedEx National LTL and FedEx Freight Corporation. After obtaining his BBA and MBA from Western Michigan University, he spent 43 years in Human Resources Management with seven different corporations after serving as an Adjutant and Personnel Officer of an Air Defense Artillery Battalion in the US Army. He spent 24 of those years as a vice president of Human Resources at four different corporations.

During his career, he was a board member and board chair of CUE, Inc, the only single purpose national organization whose mission is to assist member companies to remain union-free through the application of positive employee relations practices, San Antonio, TX; a board member and board chair of the North American Transportation Employee Relations Association, Washington, DC; a cofounder of "Freewheelers", an organization comprised of 20+ national trucking companies who meet regularly to discuss common HR practices and industry workforce issues, Birmingham, AL; a board member of Blue Ridge Conference on Leadership, Auburn University, AL; a board member of the United Way of Central Florida, Lakeland, FL; and board member and board Chair of American Red Cross, Polk County Chapter, Winter Haven, FL.

Steve and his wife live in Boone, North Carolina, where he enjoys watercolor painting, fly fishing, pistol and trap shooting, and judging BBQ contests. Steve serves on the board of directors of the Watercolor Society of North Carolina focusing on long range planning for the society.

Steve can be connected with on LinkedIn, Google+ and on Twitter at @shnewhouse.